LIVING IN
THE
POWER
OF
ONE

Making A
Difference in
A Broken World

Stan Toler
David Dean

All quotations, excerpts, and notations by Stan Toler used with permission.

Scripture quotations marked KJV are taken from the Holy Bible, authorized King James Version.
Scripture quotations marked NLT are taken from New Living Translation, used by permission of Tyndale House. The "NIV" and "New International Version" are trademarks registered in the United States Patent and Trademark Office by Biblica, Inc. Scripture quotations marked NIV, New International Version copyright by Biblica, Inc. Used by permission. Scripture quotations marked (MSG) are taken from The Message. by Eugene H. Peterson. Used by permission. Scripture quotations marked as NKJV are taken from the New King James Version by Thomas Nelson. Used by permission.

To order additional copies of this book, contact:

Address all inquiries to
David Dean
21271 Wintergreen Drive
Circleville, Ohio 43113
www.amazon.com

For Worthwhile Books
FWB Publications

Table of Contents

FOREWORD

I was highly honored when David Dean, one of my closest friends, asked me to write a foreword for his book, Living in the Power of One. I first met David in Arizona in the early 1970's when my wife and I were missionaries to Native Americans and David and his wife were pastoring a small congregation in Tucson. From the day we met, his love for the Lord and his passion to reach the unsaved were beautifully obvious. The anointing of the Holy Spirit was clearly upon his life and ministry.

As the decades have rolled by, our friendship has deepened as the Lord has given us countless opportunities to be involved in ministry together. In various leadership roles, in local church ministry, and in Great Commission outreach around the world, we have served together. Our mutual friendship with Dr. Stan Toler and Dr. John Maxwell linked our hearts even more passionately in a shared vision to see our world reached for Christ.

Based upon a lifetime of experience in obedience to our Lord's command to "make disciples", David has written a book that I consider a masterpiece. Not only does he describe the qualities of a genuine disciple, but he gives a blueprint for effective disciple-making.

Over the past several years I have heard David teach lessons from "Living the Power of One" in China, the Middle East and Northern Africa.

In fact, in Lebanon he and I taught the curriculum together.

The response has been the same everywhere - a deepened surrender and hunger for a Christ-like life empowered by the Spirit, a renewed passion to reach the lost, and a covenant with God to intentionally invest in helping others become fully devoted disciples of Christ.

If you truly desire to make a maximum eternal difference, I highly recommend David's book.

Doug Carter
Senior Vice President, EQUIP
Duluth, GA

TESTIMONIALS ABOUT LIVING IN THE POWER OF ONE

Living in the Power of One is written through the lens of obedience and commitment to building the kingdom of God. As you read you will see David's passion and heart for God and His Church. You will love this book, and it is written by a person who truly is "Living in the Power of One."

Rev. Mike Holbrook,
General Superintendent of the
Churches of Christ in Christian Union

I am so excited about this book and the teaching of *Living in the Power of One*. I believe that God has given David this message and will use it mightily to teach it for the glory of God. I believe this book will go to the nations and have a great impact. I strongly recommend everyone to read and apply it. It is a timeless gem, very powerful and it works.

George Lo
Corporate Executive in Asia

When my good friend, David Dean, handed me a manuscript for Living in the Power of One, it was several weeks before I read it. But when I did, I recognized it as a powerful tool to be used in motivating Christians around the world to make a difference for Jesus. The simple but powerful concept of one person, given completely over to the Lordship of Christ, doing their part for the kingdom, was the message we were looking for at Bethel Church.

We implemented *Living In The Power of One* through our small group ministry and our church responded extremely well. We have seen increases in attendance, first time guests, giving and a general overall excitement at Bethel Church. Living in the Power of One has been a part of this stirring of the Holy Spirit. Thank you, David, for introducing us to Living in the Power of One.

Rev. Bobby Bentley, Pastor
Bethel Congregational Methodist Church
Butler, Georgia

When Rev. David Dean welcomed the idea of traveling to the Middle East and teaching his incredible evangelistic tool, *Living In the Power of One*, to the outstanding leaders in this place in the world, we expected success because the content is excellent and our leaders there are always passionate to learn more about effective evangelism! But what happened in Beirut, Lebanon far exceeded our expectations and left us absolutely amazed like those who are dreaming. Amazingly, while the course was being taught in Lebanon, the Egyptian leaders who came for this teaching were already arranging to teach *Living in the Power of One* as soon as they departed Beirut and land in Cairo, Egypt. They would not delay. In order to gain momentum, they started immediately passing on the influential course Living in the Power of One to other leaders in their homeland. As a result, so many are making a huge difference in the heart of the Middle East because they are convinced that ONE PERSON can make a huge impact when he/she simply obeys.

Michel Khalil
President of Step Forward Global Ministries

Living In

Provided for the Toler Leadership Institute by
The Kline Institute for Evangelism & Discipleship
The Carter Institute for International Leadership

A TRIBUTE TO

DR. STAN TOLER

I will never forget the first time I met Stan Toler. We were attending college at Ohio Christian University (Circleville Bible College at that time). We were both ministry majors with a sense of God's call on our lives to serve as pastors. He came into a class dressed in a black suit carrying a brown briefcase. I could not help but think, "Who is this guy?" Little did I know, on that day, he would become one my dearest friends.

From the early days in college, we served together our entire lives. Stan was always the same whether he was serving in a mission district with a small church, serving in a large church, or serving as a General Superintendent with the Church of the Nazarene.

His love for God and his passion for the church remained the driving force in his life. He touched the world with the love and message of Jesus Christ during his lifetime. He preached in every state in the United States and over 90 countries around the world.

In addition to his preaching and teaching ministry, he was able to write over 100 books! His brother Terry remarked that, "Stan never had an unpublished thought."

I am not sure about that, but I do know that he was a rare man with a great heart and an anointed life.

During the last three years of Stan's life, I had the privilege of working closely with him to develop The Toler Leadership Institute at Ohio Christian University. We traveled together to empower leaders around the world.

One of his signature works was The Power of One. He developed this seminar to assist churches in the work of evangelism. Reaching out to lost people and introducing them to Jesus Christ was the joy of his life. It was my privilege to teach this material with and for him. During those years, he told me he had written a companion book for each of his seminars. However, he said that he had not written a companion book for The Power of One. He said that he was leaving that to me and worked with me in the writing of this book before his death from pancreatic cancer in 2017.

I have written this book as he requested. I know that he could have done it better, but I have tried to capture his heart in this work.

How fitting the title of this book is *Living In The Power of One* because if anyone ever did that, it was Stan Toler.

Stan Toler is the personification of what God can do with a life that is fully committed to making a difference in a broken world.

This book is my tribute to a great friend.

David Dean

DEDICATION

I am dedicating this book to Rev. John Cooper, a dear friend, and colleague in ministry, at the Brookside Church for 15 years. John passed away in December of 2010 unexpectedly of cancer. His life is the inspiration for this book. He has shown all of us what can happen if just one person, dedicates his/her life to making a difference in our world.

Thank you, John, for your friendship and your example to me.

David Dean

PREFACE

In the year of 2010, the Churches of Christ in Christian Union held a Global Impact Seminar in Circleville, Ohio. During this seminar, Dr. Stan Toler presented a new focus on evangelism entitled, **THE POWER OF ONE.**

Dr. Toler had developed this program to help Christians reach unchurched people and bring them to faith. When Dr. Toler served as Senior Pastor in Oklahoma, he introduced **THE POWER OF ONE** to the congregation. As a result, the church grew to over 1,000 in attendance. It was then used all over the world to mobilize Christians to share their faith with others. Where this program was used, churches grew, people came to faith in Christ, and new churches began.

This seminar made a significant impact on my life. I developed four additional aspects of the program and produced the extra material for a discipleship focus. I have continued to develop and refine the content over the last several years.

The purpose of this book is that there is power in the life of one individual, whose life is committed to God, to make a difference in our broken world.

The process begins when one person commits to touch a lost world with the love and message of Jesus Christ.

When one person reaches out to another person, others are released to share their faith as well. When others begin to share their faith, the effort starts to multiply.

This simple strategy brought great revival and growth to churches around the world. Some could say, " We could never do that in my church." Whenever one person chooses to live in **THE POWER OF ONE**, it has worked and will work in a large city setting or a rural location.

On a mission trip to Asia in March of 2011, I shared **THE POWER OF ONE** with some dear friends who were very active in building the Church in that part of the world. Their response was overwhelming. As they listened to the explanation of **THE POWER OF ONE**, they said that "*It is divine.*" During the trip, several individuals asked me to put this material in writing so they could use it to disciple other believers.

This strategy is simple and biblical. It was used in the rapid growth of the early Church and will work in every place where people commit to understand and live this concept.

LIVING IN THE POWER OF ONE means every Christian is committed to live with a:

>**Single Purpose:** Doing the will of God whatever the cost and whatever the result
>
>**Single Passion:** Knowing Christ better each day
>
>**Single Priority:** Loving God and loving others
>
>**Single Pursuit:** Pursuing biblical unity

Living In the Power of One requires commitment and discipline. However, the rewards of seeing many people begin to change the world with their one and only life will far outweigh any cost that might come with it.

Throughout this book, I will be sharing my personal experiences to help you *Live In The Power of One.*

MY PRAYER FOR YOU IS THAT YOU WILL BE ONE WHO COMMITS TO LIVING IN THE POWER OF ONE!

INTRODUCTION

For the past several years, I have had a passion for **THE POWER OF ONE** and all it could mean to the Church of Jesus Christ. It has been my joy to teach about **THE POWER OF ONE** to people all over the world. I have found where this concept is *understood and practiced,* that marvelous things happen in the kingdom of God.

Many have asked me to explain exactly what *Living In the Power of One* is and how they can become a part of a worldwide effort to reach others for Christ.

THE POWER OF ONE is a seminar that can assist a local church to develop an effective strategy for evangelism. My dear friend, Stan Toler, wrote this portion of the workbook.

Living in the Power of One adds a discipleship element to *The Power of One.* This portion of the workbook attempts to help believers grow in their faith by encouraging:

- *Every believer to get involved in the great work of evangelism and discipleship*

- *Every believer make a decision to grow in his or her faith and make a difference in our broken world*

- *Every local church makes fulfilling the Great Commission and the Great Commandment their deepest passion*

Living In

POWER OF ONE PROFILE

An Example of the Power of One

He was a quiet man, content to serve in the background. He devoted his life to serving people one at a time. He often visited those who were ill or confined to their homes. He spent many hours counseling with people who were walking through difficult experiences.

One day he called to say he had developed severe pain and was diagnosed with shingles. For several weeks, the pain intensified and grew worse. Our church family prayed that he would soon recover. One afternoon he went to the local hospital. When I saw him, he told me that he was in the worst pain of his life. After leaving the hospital my wife, Connie, and I made an appointment to receive the shingle vaccine to protect ourselves from such agony! Two weeks later, John was still in great pain, so Connie and I went to his home to have prayer. When we arrived, John was unable to get out of his chair. He was suffering terribly.

We had prayer with him, and as we left, I told Connie that I had seen that "look" before. It was the look of someone with cancer.

One week after our visit, John entered the hospital. After running tests, the doctors came into the room with the dreaded words, "John has cancer, and there is nothing you can do." We were all shocked and stunned. A few hours later, John made the crossing to another world in the early hours of a Tuesday morning!

I went to the church office and sent **ONE** email to let our church family know. I called the church together for a prayer meeting the next night.

When the service began, I was completely astounded. The church was filled with people. It was a larger crowd than I had preached to on the previous Sunday. When it came time for the memorial service, it was astonishing again. The line of people to honor Pastor John Cooper had to form inside and outside of the church. People came by weeping and asking me, "What are we going to do? He was the only reason I came to church!" That was a humbling experience for me as the Senior Pastor of the church. It was during that service that God whispered to me, "You wonder how important it is to minister to just one person at a time. See the result of **THE POWER OF ONE!**" John became an example and an inspiration of what it means to **LIVE IN THE POWER OF ONE**.

How vital is it to minister to one person at a time? Pastor John Cooper forever showed all of us what The Power of One can do!

SECTION ONE:
THE POWER OF A SINGLE PURPOSE

Living In

THE POWER OF A SINGLE PURPOSE

The single purpose for *Living in the Power of One* is *to do the will of God regardless of cost, consequence or result.*

In every situation, big or small, if our commitment is to do the will of God, we will have a sense of direction. We will never grow in our walk with the Lord until there is a commitment to do the will of God in every area of our life.

When doing the will of God regardless of cost, or consequence, you can:

- *OBEY GOD when you must stand alone*

- *OBEY GOD when you do not understand*

- *OBEY GOD when you are afraid*

- *OBEY GOD when you feel like you have little to offer*

Living In

POWER OF ONE PROFILE

David: Obeying God When You Must Stand Alone

King Saul and his army were terrified. They had hidden behind the bushes and rocks. The reason for their fear, a giant by the name of Goliath had appeared to challenge the army of Israel. Goliath came out every day, into an open area between the Philistines and the Israelites to curse God and to challenge anyone from Saul's army to fight against him. All of the soldiers, Saul included, were completely intimidated. They felt it was hopeless to compete against this giant. However, a young man named David had been sent by his father to the battlefield to take supplies to his brothers.

When he met with his brothers on the front line, his brothers did not receive him well.

> "But when David's oldest brother, Eliab, heard David talking to the men, he was angry. 'What are you doing around here anyway? He demanded. What about those few sheep you're supposed to be taking care of? I know about your pride and deceit. You just want to see the battle!'"
> 1 Samuel: 17:28 NLT

While on the front line, David heard Goliath cursing God. Hearing Goliath curse the God of heaven stirred his heart to anger. He started asking questions. King Saul heard about David's interest in Goliath, sent for him, and heard David say:

> "Don't worry about this Philistine," David told Saul. "I'll go fight him!" "Don't be ridiculous!" Saul replied. "There's no way you can fight this Philistine and possibly win! You're only a boy, and he's been a man of war since his youth."
> 1 Samuel 17:32-33 NLT

King Saul tried to convince David to use his armor to go against Goliath. It must have been a bizarre sight to see a young man, slight of build, try to put on the armor of a king that stood head and shoulders above every other man. David then told Saul he could not wear the king's armor because he had not proved them himself. This lesson is good for all of us! We do not need to put on someone else's armor to accomplish great things for God.

David picked up five round stones and headed to face the giant. As David approached Goliath, the giant laughed and mocked him. He said,

"Am I a dog that you come at me with a stick? Come over here, and I'll give your flesh to the birds and wild animals." David replied to the Philistine, "You come to me with sword, spear, and javelin, but I come to you in the name of the Lord of Heaven's Armies–the God of the armies of Israel, whom you have defiled. Today the Lord will conquer you, and I will kill you and cut off your head...and the whole world will know that there is a God in Israel".
I Samuel 17:43-46 NLT

In anger, Goliath moved forward to attack, but David used his slingshot to hurl a stone at Goliath. The stone hit the giant in the forehead and instantly killed him. What a great miracle!

However, I submit that Goliath's death was not the greatest miracle that took place on that day. The Bible says,

"When the Philistines saw that their champion was dead, they turned and ran. The men of Israel and Judah gave a great shout of triumph and rushed after the Philistines, chasing them as far as Gath."
I Samuel 17:51-52 NLT

You see, when one person steps out in obedience, even if they must stand alone, it releases an army of others who want to do the will of God. People need someone who will step forward and show them the way.

When that one person shows what God can do, others are inspired to do what they know they should have been doing all along. David is an excellent example of **LIVING IN THE POWER OF ONE!**

WHAT GIANTS ARE YOU FACING IN YOUR LIFE THAT NEED TO BE CONQUERED?

Living In

POWER OF ONE PROFILE

Abraham: Obeying God When You Do Not Understand

It was an odd command that required a degree of faith that Abraham had never demonstrated before. The command came from God and specified that Abraham was to leave his home and his family to go to a new land that God would show him. Abraham fully trusted in God, so he made plans to follow Him wherever that might lead. No doubt, Abraham faced many questions both within himself and from others. His wife, Sarah, must have asked, "But Abraham where are we going?" Abraham would have had to answer honestly and say, "I do not know." If Sarah were anything like my wife, she would have asked, "How will we know when we arrive?" Abraham again must have had to answer, "I do not know, but God will make it plain to us when we get there." It was the risk of a lifetime!

If God did not keep His promise to Abraham, this risk would end in failure and shame.

However, we know the rest of the story. God did keep His promise to Abraham and showed him a great land. God declared that the nation we now know as Israel was to be his land and to his children and generations following them. However, there remained one question still yet unanswered. Abraham and Sarah were now growing old. He was 99, and she was 90, but they had no son to pass on this inheritance to the following generations. God promised Abraham a son. A son who would be the father of a great nation.

Once again, faith in God's promise was the only thing that made any sense to Abraham.

The Bible says, *"And Abraham believed the Lord, and the Lord counted him as righteous because of his faith."* Genesis 15:6 NLT

Abraham's willingness to believe God, even when he could not understand, brought God's favor on his life and gave birth to a great nation. Ultimately, Abraham's faith and obedience brought about the birth of the Lord Jesus Christ. There are times when God asks us to do something that we do not understand.

We know that God is too wise to be mistaken. God is too good to be unkind. When we cannot trace His hand, we trust His heart. In our obedience, we will discover that God will bless our lives and bring great good to others through a faith that obeys, even when one does not understand it all.

GOD ACCOMPLISHES GREAT THINGS THROUGH THE PERSON WHO IS WILLING TO OBEY IN SPITE OF NOT UNDERSTANDING IT ALL.

Living In

POWER OF ONE PROFILE

Barnabas: Obeying God When You Are Afraid

The word had spread like wildfire. Saul of Tarsus was coming to Damascus. His purpose for coming was to destroy the small Christian community in that city. He had killed and arrested Christians living in other towns, and now he was bringing his terror to Damascus. However, something amazing happened along the way. The Bible records it like this,

> "As he was approaching Damascus on this mission, a light from heaven suddenly shone down around him. He fell to the ground and heard a voice saying to him, "Saul! Saul! Why are you persecuting me?" "Who are you, Lord?" Saul asked. And the voice replied, "I am Jesus, the one you are persecuting! Now get up and go into the city, and you will be told what you must do."
>
> Acts 9:2-6 (NLV)

This encounter with the living Christ transformed Saul's life. He abruptly quit persecuting the Christian community and instead devoted the rest of his life to preaching about the love and grace of the Lord Jesus. What an amazing transformation took place that day on the road to Damascus! When the news reached Jerusalem about Saul's conversion to Christ, the Jewish leaders were furious with him. They felt they must kill Saul because he had become a traitor.

On the other hand, the Christians were not sure that they could trust Saul. They were afraid of him. Was he telling a story about his conversion to Christ to infiltrate their ranks so that he could destroy them? This was a great dilemma for Saul. How would he be able to convince the Christians that he had experienced a life-changing conversion and that they could trust him?

To bring a resolution to this situation, God spoke to a man by the name of Barnabas. He was an influential leader in the early church. The leaders of the Christian community knew they could trust him. His very name, Barnabas, means *the son of encouragement*. Don't we all need a son of encouragement in our lives? Barnabas went to spend time with Saul to try to understand his heart. Make no mistake; Barnabas was putting his very life on the line. If Saul's claim of converting to Christ was deceptive, Barnabas was putting his life in danger. If, on the other hand, Saul had come to know Christ as Savior and Lord, Barnabas could help introduce him to the Christian community. It is easy to see why Barnabas could have been a little fearful.

Barnabas put his fear aside and went to meet with Saul. What he discovered was that Saul had indeed come to a saving knowledge of the Lord Jesus Christ. After getting to know Saul, Barnabas took him to Jerusalem to introduce him to the Christian leaders.

Barnabas put his arm around Saul, whose name was later changed to Paul, as his friend and opened the door of fellowship to the Christian community. Peter, James, and John, after listening to Barnabas and Paul determined that Paul was worthy for the ministry. Barnabas' decision to be a friend to Paul brought great blessing to the Church. Paul would later travel throughout the known world preaching the gospel.

After his arrest for his faith in Christ, he would write most of the New Testament from prison and would become the most influential Christian leader in the Gentile (non-Jewish) world.

What would have happened if Barnabas had given in to earthly fear and had not taken the risk to be a friend to the Apostle Paul? Only God knows what a loss that would have been to the entire kingdom of God. Barnabas became an example of **LIVING IN THE POWER OF ONE** by simply becoming a friend to a person in need.

WHO DO YOU KNOW THAT NEEDS A FRIEND?

Living In

POWER OF ONE PROFILE

A Boy and His Lunch: Obeying God When You Feel That You Have Little To Offer

The sun was rapidly sinking across the western horizon. A crowd of over five thousand people had gathered to listen to Jesus of Nazareth preach and teach. The disciples, realizing the people had not eaten and they were in a remote place, advised Jesus to send the crowd away so they could purchase something to eat. Jesus, then shocked His disciples when He said,

"'You feed them.' 'With what?' they asked. 'We'd have to work for months to earn enough money to buy food for all these people!' 'How much bread do you have?' he asked. 'Go and find out.'" Mark 6:37-38 NLT *"Then Andrew, Simon Peter's brother, spoke up. 'There is a young boy here with five barley loaves and two fish. But what good is that with this huge crowd?'"* John 6:8-9 NLT

"Jesus told the disciples to have the crowd sit down in groups of 50 or a hundred. Jesus then took the five loaves and two fish, looked up to heaven and BLESSED them. Then, breaking the loaves into pieces, he kept giving the bread to the disciples so they could distribute it to the people. He also divided the fish for everyone to share. They all ate as much as they wanted, and afterward the disciples picked up twelve baskets of leftover bread and fish."

Mark 6:37-43 NLT

For this miracle to take place, two things had to happen: the boy had to give his lunch to Jesus, and Jesus had to accept the boy's lunch as it was.

The boy did give his lunch to Jesus. He gave it all. He gave it willingly and gave it gladly. I believe the boy gave his lunch to Jesus because he thought Jesus was hungry. He had no idea that a miracle would take place that day. It is the same with us, when we are willing to give our little to Jesus, miracles can take place in ways that we would have never thought possible. Sometimes we hesitate to do the will of God because we feel that we have so little to offer. It is not the size of our offering that makes the difference, but the power of Christ that transforms it.

As small as it was, Jesus did receive and accept the boy's lunch. Most of us would ask the disciples, "What do you expect me to do with this?" However, Jesus took the loaves, blessed the loaves, broke the loaves and then used the loaves to feed a hungry crowd to bring glory to the Father.

When we give our lives to Christ, He blesses us, breaks us, and uses us in miraculous ways regardless of how insignificant we think we are.

Can you imagine the scene when the boy finally returned home to tell his mother that he had given his lunch to Jesus? Can you hear her groans about how she had told him not to waste his food? Can you see her face when the boy said to her that Jesus then fed over five thousand people from five loaves and two fish? Can you feel the overwhelming sense of joy that came over her as the boy pointed out the twelve men that had followed him home with baskets of leftovers for him and his family! It seems too good to be true, but the Scriptures affirm the account.

Do you feel that you have little to offer the Lord in your life? You may think that your talents and skills are so small in a world that needs to hear the good news of Christ and His salvation. May I remind you that God can take your life, however small and insignificant you think it is, and use it for His Glory!

The old song says:

Little is much when God is in it!
Labor not for wealth or fame;
There's a crown, and you can win it,
If you go in Jesus' name.[1]

The little boy becomes an example of **LIVING IN THE POWER OF ONE**.

---

[1] Little is Much When God Is In It. Lyrics At Word Music LLC. Word Music, LLC

WHEN WE GIVE WHAT LITTLE WE HAVE TO AN ALMIGHTY GOD, HE CAN BLESS AND MULTIPLY IT IN WAYS THAT WE WOULD NEVER DREAM POSSIBLE.

THE POWER OF ONE

I am only one, But still, I am one.

I cannot do everything,

But still I can do something;

And because I cannot do everything

I will not refuse to do the something that I can do.

I am only one, but I am one.

I can't do everything, but I can do something.

The something I ought to do, I can do.

And by the grace of God, I will.

I am only one, but I am one.

I cannot do everything, but I can do something.

And I will not let what I cannot do interfere with what I can do.

Edward Everett Hale

Living In

THE COMPELLING
PURPOSE OF CHRIST

Is there a single purpose that is worth giving your life to?

LIVING IN THE POWER OF ONE is, first, a call to those who are followers of the Lord Jesus Christ— to commit their lives to a single purpose.

In an age where many have become distracted by the things of this world, is it possible for people to discover the beauty of a life lived with a single purpose? To answer this question, we look to the Scripture for guidance.

The book of Hebrews was written to proclaim to all that Christ was the fulfillment of the very plan of God. Everything that went before Him was merely to point the way to Him as the perfect sin sacrifice and the perfect Savior for all who will trust Him!

Hebrews 10:5,7 NLT reads, *"That is why, when Christ came into the world, he said to God… I have come to do your will, O God…"* There, in the words of the Lord Jesus, we discover the grand purpose of His life. His greatest desire was to devote His life to do the will of the Father. *"I have come to do your will Oh God."* Hebrews 10:7 NLT

In other words, Jesus was declaring that He would bring glory to the Father and purchase full salvation for all. He lived His life with one great purpose in everything He did…*simply to do the Will of God* …everyday, in every situation, and in every dimension of life. Even when the will of God led Him to the Garden of Gethsemane and the Cross of Calvary. His purpose never faltered for He declared, *"I have come to do your will Oh God."* Hebrews 10:7 NLT

When Christians commit to the single purpose of doing the will of God, whatever the cost, consequence, or result, great things begin to take place in the Church and the world.

LIVING IN THE POWER OF ONE begins when a Christian makes a conscious decision in his or her life *to do the will of God—whatever the cost, whatever the consequence, and whatever the result.*

You see, when one makes that commitment, we no longer are talking about just an outreach program or a new emphasis to build the Church. It becomes foundational in our lives, and it becomes a way of life, which *includes* outreach and touching lost people for Christ–*a great difference!*

When we commit to do the will of God in our life whatever the cost and whatever the result, it affects every major decision: what we do, where we work, how we live, and how we minister to those around us. While we know that the will of God does not look the same for everyone, it is uniform in how we live out God's plan for spiritual growth and fruitfulness. **LIVING IN THE POWER OF ONE** is about understanding what happens when one person is committed to doing the will of God.

Even though the task may have seemed to be impossible, throughout Scripture God always has chosen one person who was committed to Him and was willing to be obedient. This person's obedience and faith always brought victory and revival.

Show me what God is doing anywhere in the world, where the Church is growing and doing great works of compassion and social justice, and it will point to some individual who is doing something in obedience to God's voice in his or her heart and life. Someone has said to God, "I'll do it!" or "I'll go."

IT ALL BEGINS WITH A COMMITMENT TO A SINGLE PURPOSE.

QUESTIONS FOR REFLECTION:

1. What do you think that Jesus meant when He said to the Father, "I have come to do your will Oh God?" How do you think that commitment influenced all His life and His ministry?

_____

_____

_____

_____

_____

_____

2. What single purpose have you committed your life to accomplish? Is it worth giving your life for it?

_____

_____

_____

_____

_____

_____

3. Do you know someone who has demonstrated a commitment to doing the will of God regardless of the cost? How does that commitment affect their lives? The lives of others? Your own life?

_____

_____

_____

_____

_____

4. Are you committed to doing the will of God regardless of the cost or consequence in your life? Why or why not?

_____

_____

_____

_____

_____

_____

Living In

GOD'S PURPOSE FOR YOUR LIFE

What does the will of God look like in your life?

The will of God for your life is to become a Disciple of Christ. A disciple of Christ is a person who desires to make a difference in our broken world.

In Matthew 28:18-20 Jesus says to His disciples:

> *"I have been given all authority in heaven and on earth. Therefore, go and make disciples of all the nations, baptizing them in the name of the Father and the Son and the Holy Spirit. Teach these new disciples to obey all the commands I have given you. And be sure of this: I am with you always, even to the end of the age."*

LIVING IN THE POWER OF ONE is a challenge to embrace the call of the Lord Jesus to discipleship in our lives.

The process of making disciples always includes two dimensions:

1. It always involves **becoming a disciple** of the Lord Jesus Christ.

2. It always involves **developing other disciples** of the Lord Jesus Christ.

Before we can ever think about reaching out to others who do not know Christ as Lord and Savior, we must focus on our own lives. We cannot teach what we do not know, and we cannot give what we do not possess.

Therefore, before we can teach others about the will of God, we must first understand what it means to be a disciple of the Lord Jesus Christ in our own life.

People Who Make an Eternal Difference Have a Sense of *ASSURANCE* About Their Salvation.

We can have an assurance of our salvation when:

- We have become aware of the fact that we *are sinners* and have a great need for a Savior: *"For everyone has sinned; we all fall short of God's glorious standard."*

Romans 3:23 NLT

- We *confess our sins* to God and trust Him to forgive our sins according to His Word: *"But if we confess our sins to him, he is faithful and just to forgive us our sins and to cleanse us from all wickedness."*

I John 1:9 NLT

- We pray *and invite the Lord Jesus* into our hearts and lives: *"Look! I stand at the door and knock. If you hear my voice and open the door, I will come in, and we will share a meal together as friends.* "Revelation 3:20 NLT

- We believe that *God forgives our sins and our past:*
  "If you openly declare that Jesus is Lord and believe in your heart that God raised him from the dead, you will be saved. For it is by believing in your heart that you are made right with God, and it is by openly declaring your faith that you are saved."
  Romans 10:9-10 NLT

- We seek to *live a new life of faith* as God helps us:
  "My old self has been crucified with Christ. It is no longer I who live, but Christ lives in me. So I live in this earthly body by trusting in the Son of God, who loved me and gave himself for me." Galatians 2:20 NLT

- We trust the Lord to *give us a new start* in life:
  "This means that anyone who belongs to Christ has become a new person. The old life is gone; a new life has begun!"
  2 Corinthians 5:17 NLT

- We determine to do *whatever it takes to be what God wants us to be:*

"So that one way or another, I will experience the resurrection from the dead! I don't mean to say that I have already achieved these things or that I have already reached perfection. But I press on to possess that perfection for which Christ Jesus first possessed me."

Philippians 3:11-12 NLT

The will of God is always that we come to a clear assurance that God, for Christ's sake, has forgiven our sins. Without this confidence, we will never be able to understand His Will.

The question that you must face today is, "Have you trusted Christ for the forgiveness of sins and have the assurance of eternal life in your heart?"

If not, why not take time today to pray asking God to do a work of grace in your life by saying a simple prayer like this:

"Lord Jesus, I know that I have sinned and fallen short of your glory in my life.
Today I invite you to come into my life and forgive my sins.

Through your completed work on the cross on my behalf, I trust you for complete forgiveness of my sins and a brand-new start in my life.

As you help me day-by-day, I want to live a life of faith and obedience in the days ahead.

I commit today to become a disciple for You, and I desire to do Your will, whatever the cost.
In Jesus name, I pray."

Amen.

If you sincerely prayed this prayer, you can rejoice that God is faithful, and He will answer your prayer. You can trust Him to forgive your sins and to make you His child through faith in the Lord Jesus Christ.

The gospel of Christ is the most wonderful news that you will ever hear. A true disciple of Christ always rejoices in the wonder of God's Grace that has forgiven their sins and completely changed the direction of their lives.

IT IS THE WILL OF GOD THAT YOU HAVE AN ASSURANCE OF SALVATION IN YOUR LIFE.

Living In

POWER OF ONE PROFILE

The Assurance of Salvation

While serving as the Senior Pastor of the Brookside Church, I often made visits to the local hospital. One afternoon, I stopped by the emergency room (ER) to see one of our members who had been involved in an accident. I approached the Information Desk and asked if I could see my friend. The ER was very busy that day. The nurse who was registering people seemed a little overwhelmed. She looked at me and said that I could see him, but I would have to wait for a little while. Patience has never been one of my strongest virtues, and it must have shown to those around me.

I looked behind the Information Desk to another young nurse who smiled and said, "Come with me, I will take you back to see him." Gratefully I accepted her offer to take me immediately to see my friend. As we were walking back to the room, I told her that my name was David Dean and that I was a Pastor.

She smiled again and said, "I know who you are. My son and I have visited your church." I said I was so glad they had come to worship with us and asked her to come again. She said she was seriously thinking about doing just that.

She wanted her son to grow up in a good church and she was giving a lot of thought to finding real purpose in her life. To my great surprise, the next Sunday morning she showed up for worship with her son.

She seemed to be quite engaged in the service. As she left the church, she said, "I will be back." From that Sunday morning, she began to come regularly. Soon she was volunteering in the Children's Department, getting involved in a Sunday School class, and making friends among the congregation.

Several months had passed, and she had become a Brookside regular. She was there every Sunday unless sick or away. At times, her husband would come. She became very involved in all that we were doing. I rejoiced to see how connected she had become.

One day, after she had been volunteering, serving, and studying, she called the Church Office and asked if she could make an appointment. We set a time, and I looked forward to talking with her even though, I will have to admit, I wondered what might be on her mind. When she arrived at the office, we sat down and chatted for a few minutes. Soon her eyes filled with tears, and I could see that she wanted to ask me a serious question.

She began by saying, "I have been attending Brookside now for several months, and we love the church." I braced for what I feared might be coming next.

She went on, "But there is something that I must know. You keep saying that we can have an assurance of our salvation, but that is something I have never had, and I so want to know how I can have that." I asked the question that I have asked scores of people before and since. I asked, "Jami, has anyone ever taken time to sit down with you, one-on-one, and share with you from the scripture what it means to be a Christian?"

She said that no one had ever done that with her even though she had attended other churches off and on, all her life. I said that it would be a great honor to do that with her. I took one of the booklets that we used at church called, *The Steps to Peace*, written by Billy Graham.[2]

We opened the booklet and we began to read together

Step 1: God loves you and wants you to experience peace and life...abundantly and eternally.

Step 2: The problem: We are separated from God because of our sins. People have tried in many ways to bridge this gap between themselves and God, but no bridge can reach God but through One.

Step 3: Jesus Christ died on the cross and rose from the grave. He paid the penalty for our sin and bridged the gap between God and all people.

Step 4: We must receive Jesus Christ as Lord and Savior and receive Him by a personal invitation.

---

[2] Steps to Peace, Billy Graham Evangelistic Association

Here is how you can receive Christ:

- *Admit your need*

I am a sinner

- *Be willing to turn from your sin*

Repent

- *Believe that Jesus Christ died on the cross and rose from the grave*

Believe

- *Through prayer, invite Jesus Christ, to come in to your heart and lead your life*

Invite

- *Receive Christ as your personal Lord and Savior*

Receive

As we finished reading through the booklet, I asked if she was ready to pray so she could have an absolute assurance of her relationship with God. She looked at me somewhat bewildered and said, "You mean I can pray right here, right now?" I assured her that she could.

We knelt beside the small couch in my office. I prayed first and then prompted her to pray in her own words. First, to tell God how sorry she was for the sins in her life.

Tears ran down her cheeks as she prayed from her heart and asked God to forgive her.

Then I prompted her to invite the Lord Jesus into her heart and life. Again, she prayed with such sincerity as she told the Lord that she wanted Him in her life.

We paused a moment after she prayed, and then I asked her a question, "Jami, do you think God would lie to you?" Horrified, she said, "Never!" I shared with her Revelation 3:20 NIV which says,

"Here I am! I stand at the door and knock. If anyone hears my voice and opens the door, I will come in and eat with that person, and they with me."

I asked her if she sincerely invited the Lord Jesus to come into her heart and life. She assured me that she had done that as honestly as she knew how to pray. I then showed her this verse again and asked, "If you have truly repented of your sins and if you have truly invited Christ into your heart, where is He right now?" She looked at me, and a heavenly light began to shine in her face as she exclaimed, "He is right here in my heart!"

We wept together. I asked her to thank God, in her own words, for what He had done. With joy and gratitude, she gave thanks to God for His Grace in her life.

As she left my office that day, she thanked me for helping her understand how to have the sweet assurance of her salvation in Christ. From that day until now, Jami has served the Lord with undying devotion. She since has led her husband, Tony, to a recommitment of his life to Christ and has brought her son up in a distinctly Christian home.

It is the will of God that we have a sweet assurance of salvation in our lives. Do you have that assurance today?

If not, I would encourage you to read *Steps To Peace* by Billy Graham, and pray for Christ to come into your life.

YOU TOO CAN HAVE THE ASSURANCE OF SINS FORGIVEN IN YOUR LIFE!

QUESTIONS FOR REFLECTION

1. What does the word "Savior" mean to you? When and how did you come to an awareness of your need of a Savior in your life?

_____

_____

_____

_____

_____

_____

2. What was your life like before you came to the knowledge of Christ as Savior?

_____

_____

_____

_____

_____

_____

3. When and where did you decide to receive Christ into your life?

_____

_____

_____

_____

_____

_____

4. What difference has knowing Christ made in your life?

_____

_____

_____

_____

_____

_____

5. Is it your desire to do the will of God whatever the cost?

_____

_____

_____

_____

_____

_____

Living In

THE Power OF ONE

DISCOVERING GOD'S PURPOSE FOR YOUR LIFE

Do you desire to grow in your faith?

Growth is a natural process of living things and people. It is normal for a baby to grow through various stages of life until that child becomes a mature individual capable of producing another life, and the cycle begins all over again.

In the same manner, those who have truly received new life from God demonstrate normal behavior by desiring to grow to maturity in Christ.

A sign I once saw in a basketball team's locker room made a lasting impression on me. The sign said, "When you are through growing...you are through." How true that is! It is sad to see people who could grow in their faith but decide not to do so.

Dynamic disciples of the Lord Jesus Christ experience spiritual growth in their lives.

The New Testament instructs every believer in Christ to *"Grow in the grace and knowledge of our Lord and Savior Jesus Christ"*.

2 Peter 3:18 NLT

Those individuals, who are growing in their faith, are committed to *DISCIPLINES* that the Spirit of God uses to nurture our growth.

The process for spiritual growth includes:

GROWING→LEARNING→MATURING→

LIVING→REACHING

When these disciplines are a regular part of a Christians life, spiritual growth begins to occur. Just as growth in the natural realm comes easily without force or pressure, so does spiritual growth occur in the depths of our soul. This growth then becomes evident to those who are around us.

IT IS THE WILL OF GOD FOR YOU TO GROW IN YOUR FAITH.

Living In

POWER OF ONE PROFILE

A Desire to Grow In Her Faith

I will never forget the first time I met her. She and her family had come to our church to attend Vacation Bible School. It was a chance meeting because I was not in the children's area often; but I was that day. I noticed the young family who looked lost in a large church complex. I introduced myself as the Senior Pastor, and we discussed the upcoming Vacation Bible School as well as the church in general. They seemed relieved that someone could help guide them through the process of the first visit to a new church. They promised they would bring their son to VBS, which began the next evening.

As parents began bringing their children to VBS the next night, I saw Amanda and her son, Rowan. We spoke briefly, and she seemed glad to see a familiar face. After taking Rowan to his class, I noticed that she was sitting alone in the lobby. She did not want to leave the campus in case Rowan needed her.

I went over to where she was sitting to begin a conversation. I asked about her spiritual journey. She told me that she was searching for a sense of purpose in her life. I asked if she had read *The Purpose Driven Life*, by Rick Warren.[3] She answered, "No, but would like to."

I told her that I had an extra copy and would gladly give her one. I went to my office, signed it, and gave the book to her as a gift. She seemed so excited and grateful that I would take the time to give this book to her.

When she returned the next night for VBS, I asked if she had read the first chapter. She looked very sad and said that she began to help with the other children in the church's kitchen the night before and somehow misplaced the book. I assured her that I had another book; but she said that she could not take it because she felt so bad because she had lost the one that I had signed for her. I contacted our church facilities manager, Sharon, to ask if she had seen the lost book. She had! I went to retrieve it. When I returned with the book, Amanda was walking to her car. I called out to her and told her that I had found her book. She was overjoyed and said she felt God was saying her life did have a purpose!

She began to read the book, take notes, and fill an entire notebook with her reflections. She came to the Church Office once a week and we discussed what she was reading. While reading the *Purpose Driven Life*, Amanda recommitted her life to Christ.

---

[3] The Purpose Driven Life, Copyright 2002 by Rick Warren Zondervan Publishing House, Grand Rapids, Michigan 49530

She began to grow in her faith. She demonstrated a desire to know more about the Lord and the purpose He had for her life.

When she completed the book, she asked if I had another book she could read. I recommended she begin to read *Becoming a Contagious Christian*[4] so she could reach out to her unsaved friends. She began reading the book and attending a mid-week small group Bible study.

She started volunteering and serving the church in every way she could. She enrolled her son in the Christian School at our church and began to help as an Aide. She testified and told her story of faith to everyone who would listen to her.

Amanda grew in her faith during those days in a way I have rarely seen in over 40-years of ministry.

As she grew in her faith, she began to feel convicted of her living arrangements with her boyfriend. In early December, I felt prompted by the Lord to offer to give her a wedding on Christmas Eve, following our Christmas Eve candlelight communion service. She could not believe it and asked me to speak with her boyfriend, Drew.

When I spoke to Drew, he teared up and said he could not believe we would do that. I assured him was serious. The next week Drew made an appointment to see me and told me he wanted to become a Christian because of the love and warmth he had felt in our church as well as the change he had seen in Amanda's life.

---

[4] Becoming A Contagious Christian, Copyright 1994 by Bill Hybels, Zondervan Publishing House, Grand Rapids, Michigan 49530

He also told me that he had talked to one of his friends the week before and told him he did not believe in weddings because they were just a way for churches to make money! He said, "You have taken away every excuse I have used not to become a Christian." We prayed together and Drew invited the Lord Jesus into his heart and life.

On Christmas Eve, the Church came together for one of the most beautiful weddings I have ever seen. They became a Christian husband and wife that night and established a Christian home for their son, Rowan. Some months after the wedding, Amanda and Drew moved to Texas. Drew received a new job offer and now is a very successful construction manager. Amanda is still volunteering in her church and community. She loves to tell her story of how God not only brought purpose to her life but also completed it with a Christian family. They now have a second son. They had thought about naming him, Brookside, after the Church, but felt that might be a little strange. They settled on the name of David. Imagine that!

YOU NEVER KNOW WHAT GOD WILL DO IN YOUR LIFE WHEN YOU COMMIT TO GROWING IN YOUR FAITH.

QUESTIONS FOR REFLECTION:

1. Do you have a deep desire to grow as a Christian in your faith?

_____

_____

_____

_____

_____

_____

2. What steps are you taking to allow the Spirit of God to produce growth in your life?

_____

_____

_____

_____

_____

_____

3. How would you describe your commitment to the five disciplines of growing Christians?

   Growing, Learning, Maturing, Living, Reaching

_____

_____

_____

_____

_____

_____

4. Which of these disciplines do you need to focus on to grow as a Christian today?

_____

_____

_____

_____

_____

_____

_____

HOW DO YOU DISCOVER THE WILL OF GOD FOR YOUR LIFE?

Often, I have heard it said, "Oh, I wish I could just begin life all over again and this time do it right!"

The truth is that when we believe in the Lord Jesus Christ, we are made new through His wonderful power and grace. The Bible declares,

"This means that anyone who belongs to Christ has become a new person. The old life is gone; a new life has begun!"   2 Corinthians 5:17 NLT

The marvelous truth is that when God has forgiven our sins and mistakes of the past, He also gives us a brand-new start.

People may not forget the things we did and there are times, we cannot forget the mistakes of the past.

The truth is that God has forgiven our past and has given us a new beginning through His wonderful grace.

Could there be any more wonderful message for all of us—to know that God's grace can give us a fresh start in life as we follow Him?

As we trust Christ as Savior, we receive so many things that are new in our lives. Dr. John Maxwell in his book, *Firm Foundation*, mentions these new beginnings:

WE HAVE A NEW:

- *Confidence*:
  "I have written this to you who believe in the name of the Son of God; so that you may know you have eternal life."

  1 John 5:13 NLT

- *Communication*:
  "Once Jesus was in a certain place praying. As he finished, one of his disciples came to him and said, "Lord, teach us to pray..."

  Luke 11:1 NLT

- *Challenge*:
  "This means that anyone who belongs to Christ has become a new person. The old life is gone; a new life has begun!"

  2 Corinthians 5:17 NLT

- *Guidebook*:
  "All Scripture is inspired by God and is useful to teach us what is true and to make us realize what is wrong in our lives. It corrects us when we are wrong and teaches us to do what is right."

  2 Timothy 3:16 NLT

- *Freedom:*
  "But if we are living in the light, as God is in the light, then we have fellowship with each other, and the blood of Jesus, his Son, cleanses us from all sin."   1 John 1:7 NLT

- *Opportunity:*
  "And I am praying that you will put into action the generosity that comes from your faith as you understand and experience all the good things   we   have   in   Christ."
  Philemon 6 NLT

- *Family:*
  "Let us think of ways to motivate one another to acts of love and good works. And let us not neglect our meeting together, as some people do, but encourage one another, especially now that the day of his return is drawing near."

  Hebrews 10: 24-25 NLT

- *Power:*

  "But you will receive power when the Holy Spirit comes upon you. And you will be my witnesses,   telling   people   about   me everywhere—in Jerusalem, throughout Judea, in Samaria, and to the ends of the earth."

  Acts 1:8 NLT

- *Direction:*

  "Don't copy the behavior and customs of this world, but let God transform you into a new person by changing the way you think. Then you will learn to know God's Will for you, which is good and pleasing and perfect."

  Romans 12:1-2 NLT

- *View:*

  "And we know that God causes everything to work together for the good of those who love God and are called according to his purpose..."

  Romans 8:28 NLT

- *Relationship:*

  "You are my friends if you do what I command..."

  John 15:14 NLT

Dr. Maxwell also said in his book, *Firm Foundation*, "You are now part of a wonderful adventure...the new life in Christ. At last, you have found an eternal friend, Jesus Christ. The new life you have in Him is described in the Bible in a variety of ways. You are now 'a new person' with a 'new heart' and a 'new life.' The Bible also portrays the believer as one who was dead in sin but brought back to life. You are alive unto God." In Christ, we become new persons through His Grace.

YOU HAVE BECOME A NEW PERSON IN CHRIST!

QUESTIONS FOR REFLECTION:

1. Have you ever longed for a new beginning in your life? Are there things in your life that you wished you could just forget?

2. What do you think it means when the Bible says that we have become new persons in Christ...the old life is gone, and a new life has begun?

3. Which of the new gifts that God has given us in this new life is most meaningful to you? Which one is most difficult to understand?

4. Will you pause right now to give thanks to God for His wonderful Grace that brings pardon for your sins of the past and hope for the new life ahead?

People Who Make an Eternal Difference Search for the Will of God for Their Lives

Many individuals have said that doing the will of God is not as difficult as *knowing* the will of God. There is no doubt that we must know God's will if we are going to be committed to doing it.

Discovering the will of God, at times, can be somewhat challenging, but God has promised that if we seek Him with all of our hearts, that we can find Him and know His will.

Those who want to make a difference in our world, have a heartfelt desire to know the will of God. Therefore, they incorporate habits that will give God an opportunity to reveal Himself and His will to them.

We discover God's will, as we are faithful in using spiritual disciplines.

Dr. Greg Ogden in his book, *Discipleship Essentials,*[5] mention ten of the spiritual disciplines that assist in discovering the Will of God for our lives.

- *PRAYER*: Simply talking to God each day and about every situation

- *BIBLE READING*: The Bible is God's inspired Word to us today

---

[5] Ogden, Greg., Discipleship Essentials: A Guide to Building Your Life in Christ

- *DEVOTIONAL READING*: Allowing God to speak through others to you

- *PERSONAL WORSHIP*: Expressing our love for God in our personal lives

- *PUBLIC WORSHIP*: Gathering with other believers in the church

- *BAPTISM*: Declaring your faith to the world

- *COMMUNION*: Remembering the price paid for our salvation

- *SERVING*: Discovering the ministry that God has planned for you

- *STEWARDSHIP*: Giving of one's time, talent and treasure to the Lord

- *WITNESSING*: Sharing the love of God with others

As we commit ourselves to these disciplines, we can be certain that God will reveal His will to us. Once we discover God's will, then He will empower us to do it.

One of the more significant aspects of discovering the will of God for our lives is to discover our spiritual *S.H.A.P.E.*!

What is your spiritual shape? Rick Warren, in his classic book, *The Purpose Driven Life,*[6] has the clearest definition of what this means. The word shape is an acronym for discovering our:

---

[6] Rick Warren, Purpose Driven Life: Publisher: Zondervan; Grand Rapid, Michigan

S: *Spiritual Gifts* give you an answer to *what* you do in ministry

H: *Heart* gives you a focus on *where* you do ministry

A: *Abilities* give you a direction as to what *kind* of ministry you do

P: *Personality* gives you an answer as to how you *best do* your ministry

E: *Experience* gives you an answer as to how *you help others* in your ministry[7]

There are foundational truths that you should know as you begin this exciting journey to discover your S.H.A.P.E. (See 1 Corinthians 12)

What is a spiritual gift and what does it have to do with discovering God's will in your life?

A spiritual gift is a significant ability given to Christians by the Holy Spirit to build God's Church.

What does your spiritual heart have to do with discovering God's will for your life?

Your spiritual heart is the bundle of interests, desires, hopes, and dreams that the Lord gives you.

What are abilities as it relates to discovering God's will for your life?

---

[7] Rick Warren, Purpose Driven Life: Publisher: Zondervan; Grand Rapid, Michigan

A God given talent that you must develop for ministry.

What does personality have to do with discovering God's will for your life?

Your personality is unique and makes you different from everyone else. It affects how you see yourself, others and life in general. It also affects how you relate to others in ministry.

What experiences you have gone through have to do with discovering God's will for your life?

Experiences in life develop you for ministry. God can take all of your experiences, good or bad, and use them for His Glory.

GOD MADE YOU THE WAY YOU ARE FOR A REASON AND GREAT PURPOSE.

Living In

THE *Power* OF ONE

POWER OF ONE PROFILE

A Purpose to Do the Will of God

The Brookside Church offered a quarterly membership class for individuals who wanted to join the church. We taught new members what it meant to know Christ, grow in Christ, serve Christ, and share Christ. These individuals were encouraged to discover a ministry. One of the individuals who took that class was Lana.

Lana was a very talented young woman who worked as a nurse at a local hospital. She, along with her friend, Jami, wanted to do something to make a difference in the church and their community. At the end of the course, I asked her and Jami, (who also was a nurse); if they had any thought, of what kind of ministry they would like to do. They both smiled and said that they wanted to give some consideration on how they could offer a ministry in the medical field.

About a week later, I approached them with what I thought was a brilliant idea.

I suggested they set up a wellness clinic in the church foyer once a month, check people for blood pressure and various other vital signs. They both said, "David, we love you, but that is not it!" They told me they wanted to start a free medical clinic for the working poor who had no insurance.

A little surprised by their boldness, I asked if they had ever started a clinic before. They said, "No!" I asked if they had any idea of how to start. They again said, "No!" I asked if they had a place to start a medical clinic. The answer again was, "No!" Finally, I asked the $64,000 question, do you have any money? Answer was, "No!" I told them they had a big dream, and we would need to pray about it together.

A few weeks later, Lana called to tell me that there was an emergency room doctor at the hospital that had been a part of starting medical clinics all across the state of Ohio. She asked if they should talk to him. I said, "Absolutely!"

As they began to hold regular conversations with this physician, he told them of places where he had been a part of establishing medical clinics. They began by visiting other clinics to understand how they began, how they functioned, and how they operated.

After visiting a number of these sites, they both came to me and presented the plan of establishing a free medical clinic in Chillicothe, Ohio. I asked if they had a location to begin. They said, "No, but we're still praying."

In answer to their prayers, an employee of the city heard they were looking for a place for a medical clinic.

A government building had some rooms set up as medical exam rooms, but they had no use for them. They were going to give the equipment away because they felt that they had no use for it. Lana and Jami inquired about the rooms and the equipment, and to their utter surprise, they were told that if they were going to open a medical clinic for the working poor that they could use both the equipment and the rooms AT NO CHARGE!

They were told to come set-up their registration tables and use the facility! It was a breakthrough of enormous proportions! Now having a plan, a facility, and the blessing of the County Commissioners, they were able to form a Board and search for volunteers.

An orientation meeting was scheduled for anyone interested in helping with this new clinic. To their surprise, over 200 people came for training to participate in this new ministry. People came from many different churches and vocations: nurses, doctors, children workers, registration volunteers, chaplains, and set-up crews.

Shortly after the orientation meeting, Hope Clinic of Ross County Ohio was established. Since that opening night, the clinic has been open every Monday. Hope Clinic has over 60 medical professionals volunteering their services to those in need. The Clinic also has added a dental clinic, optical clinic, a counseling center, food distribution, and referrals to specialists at the local hospital—all at much-reduced rates.

They now lease their own building, have sophisticated medical equipment, and money in the bank to provide the needed services for years to come. A second location in a nearby city has been established as well.

How amazing is that? You never know what will come to fruition in a person's life when they make an effort to discover their ministry and to follow the Lord's leading, even when it seems to be impossible.

WHEN WE COMMIT TO DOING GOD'S WILL HE OFTEN WILL WORK MIRACLES TO SEE IT ACCOMPLISHED.

Discovering the will of God can be a rather complicated process. One of the great books that I have read about this process is: *First Steps: One-On-One Discipleship,*[8], by Pastor Grant Edwards of the Springfield Fellowship Christian Church in Springfield, Ohio.

In this excellent book, Pastor Edwards gives some wonderful suggestions for discovering God's will.

In a section of the book entitled, *God's Will*, he states that God has a plan for your life and, as you follow that design, you will find joy.

Pastor Edwards advises those who are seeking to discover God's Will must build their lives on a relationship with God and faith in God.

He also teaches us God's will is progressive. God reveals His will to us progressively through meaningful ways, which include:

Specific guidance when the decision is important.

***Through* our calling and spiritual gifts** and in

***Asking* for wisdom** in faith for the knowledge of His will.

Pastor Edwards says *"God's will is confirmed in our lives through a number of avenues: the Bible, circumstances, others, and an inner peace from the Holy Spirit.*

In order to determine if something is the will of God for your life, we must develop a process of discernment.

---

[8] First Steps, One-on-One Discipleship, Copyright 2002, Specificity Publications, Third Edition 2006

This process involves understanding biblical principles, the wisdom of other Christians, what the Spirit personally is saying to you, and the correct circumstances.

Usually, as you seek God, the cycle of confirmation listed above will increase in intensity, affirming your faith that the idea is God's Will. You will find more and more biblical passages that agree, other Christians will speak words to confirm, and the Spirit's conviction will increase.

The idea transforms into a yearning so intense that you will have the faith to overcome any negative circumstances that may keep you from accomplishing it" (*First Steps: One on One Discipleship*).[7]

IT IS A GREAT JOY TO DISCOVER THE WILL OF GOD IN YOUR LIFE.

QUESTIONS FOR REFLECTION:

1. Which is more difficult for you: discovering God's will for you or doing it, and why?

_____

_____

_____

_____

_____

_____

2. Which of the spiritual disciplines are part of your life today?

_____

_____

_____

_____

_____

_____

3. Which of the spiritual disciplines are most difficult for you, and why?

_____

_____

_____

_____

_____

_____

4. What is your spiritual S.H.A.P.E.?

S: _____

H: _____

A: _____

P: _____

E: _____

5. Will you commit to these spiritual disciplines to allow God to speak to your heart about His will for your life?

_____
_____
_____
_____
_____
_____

SECTION TWO:
THE POWER OF A SINGLE
PASSION

Living In

THE POWER OF A SINGLE PASSION

The single passion for **Living in the Power of One** is, *"know Christ in the power of His resurrection and in the fellowship of His sufferings"* Philippians 3:10 NKJV.

The more we come to know Christ in our spiritual journey, the more our hearts will be broken for lost people. Reaching out to lost people does not come naturally for any of us. It is as we grow in our knowledge of Him and experience His power that we will reach out to those in our circle of influence. It is as we understand the fellowship of His suffering that we are willing to suffer along with Him even if that means rejection and insults from those we are trying to reach.

Living In

THE *Power*

OF ONE

KNOWING CHRIST

How well do you know the Lord Jesus Christ?

The Apostle Paul spoke of his passion for knowing Christ in a more personal way when he said to the Philippian Church:

> *"I once thought these things were valuable, but now I consider them worthless because of what Christ has done. Yes, everything else is worthless when compared with the infinite value of knowing Christ Jesus my Lord. For his sake I have discarded everything else; counting it all as garbage, so that I could gain Christ and become one with him.*
>
> *I no longer count on my own righteousness through obeying the law; rather, I become righteous through faith in Christ. For God's way of making us right with himself depends on faith.*

I want to know Christ and experience the mighty power that raised him from the dead. I want to suffer with him, sharing in his death, so that one way or another I will experience the resurrection from the dead. I don't mean to say that I have already achieved these things or that I have already reached perfection. But I press on to possess that perfection for which Christ Jesus first possessed me. No, dear brothers and sisters, I have not achieved it, but I focus on this one thing: Forgetting the past and looking forward to what lies ahead, I press on to reach the end of the race and receive the heavenly prize for which God, through Christ Jesus, is calling us."

Philippians 3:7-14 NLT

Can you hear the passion in the words of the great Apostle? The driving passion in his life was not worldly success, great titles, or great wealth. It was to know Christ personally, intimately, and deeply. The ministry of the Apostle Paul flowed out of his deep fellowship with God.

He did not do ministry in order to have fellowship with God, but instead, he did ministry out of his fellowship with Christ.

An important part of discipleship is knowing Christ in a personal and intimate way. We seem to be so busy that we do not take the time to come to a personal knowledge of the Lord Jesus.

This fellowship is more than just taking a few moments each day to read the Bible or to pray. It is a fellowship born out of a sincere desire for God and an earnest longing to know Him more.

This passion for knowing Christ brought Paul to the place where he declared that to know Him was greater than anything else in life.

In his, EQUIP[9] resource materials, Dr. John Maxwell states that those who desire to know God and to do great things for God have made the following choices.

They have:

- *Committed their lives to one purpose*

- *Removed every hindrance from their lives*

- *Placed themselves at God's disposal*

- *Learned to prevail in prayer*

- *Become students of God's word*

- *Chosen to serve God and others*

- *Discovered and are using their spiritual gifts*

- *The desire to help others come to Christ, grow in Christ, and be an example for others.*

- *Desire to live in the favor and blessing of God*

- *A vital message to share with others*

- *A great faith in God expecting Him to do great things*

---

[9] EQUIP, John C. Maxwell, https://maxwellcenter.com/partner/equip/

As we grow in our knowledge of the Lord Jesus Christ, we are committed to doing the will of God and experiencing His power in our lives.

THOSE WHO WANT TO MAKE AN ETERNAL DIFFERENCE IN OUR WORLD WANT TO KNOW CHRIST IN A DEEPLY PERSONAL WAY.

QUESTIONS FOR REFLECTION:

1. Is there a desire in your heart to know Christ better?
   How well do you think you know Him right now?

   _____

   _____

   _____

   _____

   _____

   _____

   _____

2. How do you think an individual grows in the knowledge
   of Christ?

   _____

   _____

   _____

   _____

   _____

   _____

3. Which one of the many choices mentioned by John Maxwell
   are you doing well in right now? Which one do you need to
   improve?

   _____

   _____

   _____

   _____

   _____

   _____

4. What steps will you take to get to know Christ better in your life?

_____

_____

_____

_____

_____

_____

_____

Living In

KNOWING CHRIST IN HIS POWER

Those Who Want To Make an Eternal Difference Want to Know Christ in the Power of His Resurrection

The Apostle Paul speaks of his great passion for knowing the power of Christ in his life. He identifies the source of this power as the Holy Spirit.

In I Corinthians 6:14 NIV he declares, *"By His power, God raised the Lord from the dead, and He will raise us also."* In I Corinthians 6:14 NLT it states, *"And God will raise us from the dead by his power, just as he raised our Lord from the dead."*

Jesus declared in Acts 1:8 NLT,

> *"But you will receive power when the Holy Spirit comes upon you. And you will be my witnesses, telling people about me everywhere—in Jerusalem, throughout Judea, in Samaria, and to the ends of the earth."*

The secret to knowing Christ in the power of His resurrection is to be filled with the Holy Spirit.

Jesus made this abundantly clear as He taught His disciples about the person and work of the Holy Spirit.

We find some of the clearest and best teaching about the Holy Spirit in the Gospel of John, Chapters 14-16. In these chapters, Jesus makes it clear that the Holy Spirit would come to abide with us.

Jesus commanded His disciples to wait in the city of Jerusalem in Luke, Chapter 24:49 NLT: *"And now I will send the Holy Spirit, just as my Father promised. But stay here in the city until the Holy Spirit comes and fills you with power from heaven."*

1. Notice the *ones* He addressed:

   His Disciples

2. Notice the *reason* for this command:

   His Disciples were weak

3. Notice the *promise* He gave:

   His Disciples would be filled with power

His disciples were to wait in Jerusalem until the Holy Spirit empowered them for the work of ministry. Jesus made it clear as to what they were to do. They were to tarry in Jerusalem until they were filled with power from on high. They were not to begin ministry or try to reach the world until they had experienced the dynamic power of being filled with the Holy Spirit.

Again, the Apostle Paul wrote:

"Don't be drunk with wine, because that will ruin your life. Instead be filled with the Holy Spirit."

Ephesians 5:18 NLT

The power of the Holy Spirit is available to all believers. People who really want to make an eternal difference in the world seek to experience the mighty power of God in their lives. The sanctifying work of the Spirit of God brings the power of a pure heart.

A PURE HEART empowers a believer to:

- Live a *victorious life*
- Live a *holy life*
- And, *do the work of ministry*

The Holy Spirit provides the power to minister to a broken world by entrusting us with spiritual gifts and giving us the ability to use these gifts.

The Holy Spirit gives us power to do the work of ministry which includes:

- Praying
- Witnessing
- Leading
- Preaching and teaching
- Admonishing and counseling
- Showing mercy
- Showing hospitality
- Working with our hands

- Sharing with lost people
- Music
- Believing
- Enduring
- Suffering
- Overcoming the evil one
- Obeying

If there is a hunger in your heart for a deeper work of God's grace in your life or there is a longing for more power in your life, please consider the following steps:

1. *Acknowledge* **your need** for the power of the Holy Spirit in your life.

2. *Surrender* **your life** to the Lordship of Christ.

3. **Ask God to** *purify* **your heart** from all sin.

4. **Ask God to** *fill* **you** with the Holy Spirit.

5. *Believe* **that God hears** and answers your prayer.

6. *Claim* **the promise of God** to fill you with His Holy Spirit in sanctifying power.

7. *Seek* **God for a daily renewal** of the Holy Spirit in your life.

8. *Learn* **to trust God for His Power** in every situation you face.

YOU TOO CAN KNOW CHRIST IN THE POWER OF HIS RESURRECTION!

Living In

POWER OF ONE PROFILE

Knowing Christ in the Power of His Resurrection

Early in my ministry, I attended a church growth conference in Denver, Colorado. I went with a very immature and selfish motive—to learn the secret of building a big church. The secret, according to the various speakers, was to have a broken heart for lost people. This message was not what I had expected it to be. I thought the secret was in some great promotional idea; however, God spoke to me during that conference.

One of the speakers preached a sermon entitled, *"Highways, Hedges and Buses."* It was a sermon about going into our communities inviting people to come to church on a church bus. I knew, even at that time, that the church bus was only a tool for a season of time, but the lasting truth was that we needed to go into our communities with a broken heart sharing the love of Jesus.

The speaker told a story about the early years of his ministry. There was a time when he seemed to be powerless for God. He tried many different things, but nothing seemed to work. He was very discouraged and ready to give up on the work of ministry. However, one night he heard a great man of God preach about being filled with the Spirit of God. The preacher said that believers could experience the power that Jesus spoke about in Acts 1:8.

He came home determined to seek for the fullness of God's Spirit and to know the power of God in his life.

He spent an evening alone reading the Bible and praying. His earnest and sincere prayer was that God would fill him with the Holy Spirit and give him the power to do the work of ministry. Around 3:00 AM, while he was kneeling before God, the sweet presence of God settled on his heart. He felt his heart strangely warmed and sensed a deep peace that God had heard and answered his prayer. The next Sunday as he went to his pulpit to preach, it felt so different. There seemed to be power in his words that he had never experienced before—a power from on high that moved people to obedience to God's call on their lives. The church soon became one of the most influential churches in the nation. Thousands came to know Christ and a great church developed.

He said that knowing Christ in the power of His resurrection was a privilege available to every believer and every servant of God. He declared in sermon, "The power of the Holy Spirit is the difference in having an ineffective life for Christ or being fruitful and advancing the kingdom of God."

It is possible to know Christ, not only as our Savior, but we can know Him in the power of His resurrection. The power of a Spirit-filled life.

What about you? Do you long for the power of God to be present in your life? The Bible promises that this is for all of those who will seek Him with all of their hearts.

QUESTIONS FOR REFLECTION:

1. From what you read in the Scripture, how important do you think that the infilling of the Spirit is in the life of the believer?

_____

_____

_____

_____

_____

_____

2. What made the difference in the lives of the disciples before Pentecost and after Pentecost? What kind of difference did it make?

_____

_____

_____

_____

_____

_____

3. Do you feel that your life is marked by power or by weakness?

_____

_____

_____

_____

_____

_____

4. Do you have a passion for knowing Christ in the power of His resurrection or are you satisfied to live where you are?

_____

_____

_____

_____

_____

_____

_____

Living In

KNOWING CHRIST IN HIS SUFFERING

Those Who Want to Make an Eternal Difference Want to Know Christ in the Fellowship of His Suffering

It is one thing for us to talk about wanting to know Christ personally and another to know Him in the power of His resurrection. Many Christians would gladly decide to do those things. However, when Paul declares that it was his passion to know Christ, not only in the power of His resurrection but in the fellowship of His suffering, a line is drawn.

When we think of the sorrows that Jesus experienced and the suffering He endured, it is unthinkable from a human perspective that anyone would want to know that kind of suffering. However, from a spiritual perspective, a full knowledge of Christ without considering the things He suffered is incomplete.

It is important to recognize that none of us can fully experience all the suffering that Jesus endured.

He took on Himself the pain of our sins as well as the sins of the whole world.

No other person could ever bear that kind of suffering, nor does God ever ask this of any other person.

However, there were things that Jesus suffered as He walked the journey of life that we may encounter in our lives:

- Being Misunderstood by Others
- Being Rejected
- Physical Exhaustion from Doing Good
- Weight of Compassion
- Grief
- Disappointment In Others
- Living in Poverty
- Others Who Would Not Believe
- Betrayal
- Surrendering To the Will of God
- Physical Pain
- Physical Death

We understand that Jesus did not live an easy life, nor did He promise an easy life to His disciples. That is why we must understand and experience the fullness of the Holy Spirit so that we may endure suffering in His name.

Living In

THE *Power* OF **ONE**

POWER OF ONE PROFILE

Knowing Christ in the Fellowship of His Suffering

She was without question, one of the sweetest girls in our entire high school. She was always dressed perfectly and appropriately. She possessed a meek and quiet spirit and was entirely devoted to the Lord Jesus Christ. Jackie was a picture of a young person who had it all.

After graduating High School, she enrolled at Circleville Bible College, now Ohio Christian University. While there, she met a life-long friend of mine, Tom Amlin. It was not long after that initial meeting that they fell in love and made plans to marry. Tom had felt God calling him into the ministry. Jackie said yes to both Tom and God. She realized that in saying yes to both that it would mean that she would give her life to the work of ministry.

After serving the Lord in central Ohio for several years and having two children, they sensed God leading them to Tucson, Arizona.

They fell in love with the Southwest and with Arizona in particular. While there, both of their lives would take a drastic turn. While playing softball at a church youth camp, Jackie fell twice while running to a base. They wondered what was happening, so they sought medical advice. When Jackie was 32, she was diagnosed with Multiple Sclerosis, an incurable and heart-rending disease. Her husband, Tom, tells the details of the story in his excellent book, *"In Sickness and in Health."* [10]

From the age of 32, Jackie began to deteriorate from a healthy, vibrant young mother, to a person confined to a wheelchair and ultimately a nursing home where she had to be cared for by others. I watched Tom and Jackie during those years. For many of us who had known them for years, it was heartbreaking to see what was taking place. However, through it all, she did not complain or lose her faith. The more she suffered, the more she blessed others. When asked how she was doing, her standard answer was always, "I'm fine!"

In spite of Jackie's illness, God called them back to Ohio and then ultimately to the Southwest Indian Ministry Center in Phoenix, Arizona as missionaries. She traveled with her husband and gave testimony to the love and grace of God even though her health was failing. Her smile never faded, and her praise for the Lord never ceased. During those years, she began to understand what it meant to *"know Christ in the fellowship of His suffering."*

---

[10] In Sickness and in Health: A Love Story, Copyright 2017 by Thomas Amlin, Dust Jacket Media Group

It is one thing to serve the Lord when everything is good, but quite another when it involves suffering and hardship that you cannot explain.

As her earthly life began to fade, her testimony only grew stronger. As the day of her departure from this life grew near, she told those who were around her, "I am going home." On May 28, 2015, Jackie went home to be with the Lord at the age of 64. I am confident that a special reward awaited her; her heavenly Father was welcoming her home. She had completed her life's mission and was now at home with the Lord forever. Early in life, Jackie wrote a mission that she wanted to characterize her life. As you read her own words, you begin to understand that she fulfilled that mission in every way. Jackie is an example of *Living in the Power of One* in a time of suffering.

Jackie's Life Mission Statement:

"I would like for the Holy Spirit to make my introverted personality traits to become strong and extroverted in spreading the Gospel of Jesus. I want to be a good wife, a loving mother, a good daughter, and a good sister. I always want to be a good example to my daughter and son so they can see Christ can meet every need. I want to be a good friend to those around me, and when I leave this world, I want people to be able to say, 'She walked the race, fought a good fight, finished the course, and kept the faith.'"

We too, can know Christ in the fellowship of His suffering when:

We choose to serve Him regardless of what we face in doing so.

We follow Him gladly, and when we encounter things in our world that are hard and difficult, we endure knowing that we come to understand the heart of Christ more as we suffer some of the same things that He suffered for us.

Make no mistake about it, those who follow Christ will not always find others applauding their decision or affirming them in what they do. When times of opposition arise, we can turn our hearts to the Savior, asking Him to help us endure them. As we experience the hardships that come with following Christ, we can then better understand the price He paid for our redemption. As we know how He suffered for us, we can then be willing to endure suffering for His name.

As we walk through the sufferings of life and because He has already experienced the hardships we experience, we can trust Him to enable us to walk through these things victoriously. His Grace, Companionship, and Strength become the means of our being able to face the sufferings of life triumphantly!

We allow our hearts to be broken with the things that break the heart of God.

At times, we think that the worst suffering we can endure is suffering ourselves. Upon examining the life of the Lord Jesus, we discover that the most significant source of suffering for Him was the suffering *others were experiencing.*

When we see people as Jesus saw them and when we are willing to allow our hearts to be broken, it is in that moment that we come to know Christ in the fellowship of His suffering.

There are so many broken people in our world and so many needs that it can be overwhelming at times. Often, we think to ourselves, "What can I do in the face of such need?"

Knowing Christ in the fellowship of His suffering becomes the great motivation to reach out to others in Jesus' name.

Living In

THE *Power*

OF ONE

POWER OF ONE PROFILE

Coming to Know Christ in a Time of Great Suffering

Joe was a very gifted and talented man. He had reached an executive level position at a trucking company in Chillicothe, OH. Life was good with only a promise of getting better.

He began having some minor chest pain, so the doctor suggested he go to a specialist at an out-of-town hospital for a heart catheterization. As they took him in, little did he know, when he awoke, his entire life would be dramatically different. The doctor began the procedure; he found that there were severe problems in his heart that required immediate open-heart surgery. The surgery was successful. However, in the night, something went wrong. The sutures broke loose, and he went into cardiac arrest. Joe actually "died" that night. The doctors continued to work with him, and eventually,

Joe came back to life. During the time of his unconsciousness, the heart was unable to pump the blood effectively to his hands and legs. In order to save his life, the doctors had to amputate.

When Joe awakened from this traumatic surgery, he discovered that he had no legs and no fingers. This was quite a shock. During the days that followed, my friend, Rev. Dan Bennett, led Joe and his wife, Donna to a saving knowledge of Christ. Both Joe and Donna knew that they had a long journey ahead of them. However, they also discovered that God's grace was sufficient for them and that Brookside Church would be there to help all along the way.

Joe began to grow in grace and the knowledge of the Lord. He and his wife, Donna, became part of the Brookside Church family. As the months began to pass, Joe said that he wanted to play golf again. He also had a desire to tell his story to whomever would listen. The story was about the grace and goodness of God enabling him to live victoriously despite pain and loss. He traveled to several churches to tell his story with Donna by his side. He did indeed learn to play golf again and often beat many of his friends!

He also felt a need and a burden to begin *a walking ministry* at Brookside Church. Imagine, the man with prosthetic legs, no fingers, and a world turned upside down, challenging others to begin to walk for their health! This ministry flourished during the rest of the years of Joe's life. He became a testimony of what a life can be, even in the middle of unspeakable suffering and tragedy.

Joe Bowsher forever proved that it is possible to bless others even while going through agonizing pain and suffering.

YOU CAN BE A BLESSING TO OTHERS EVEN IN TIMES OF SUFFERING.

During the mid-1990's a great movement began under the leadership of Coach Bill McCartney called, Promise Keepers. This was an effort to bring men, from all walks of life together to worship God and to commit to becoming Godly men. It was a powerful influence on the lives of thousands of men, including mine.

I was brought face to face with my own need to know Christ in a more intimate way as I attended these conferences.

One of the worship songs that was sung was, *Knowing You, Jesus*, written by Graham Kendrick. The lyrics struck a deep chord in my heart as thousands of men sang together:

All I once held dear, built my life upon
All this world reveres and wars to own
All I once thought gain I have counted loss
Spent and worthless now, compared to this

Now my heart's desire is to know you more
To be found in you and known as yours
To possess by faith what I could not earn
All-surpassing gift of righteousness

Oh, to know the power of your risen life
And to know You in Your sufferings
To become like you in your death, my Lord
So, with you to live ad never die

It was during that season of my life I made a decision to make my greatest passion to know Christ better each day.
That passion has brought a sense of joy and power to my life that I had never known before.

HOW WELL DO YOU KNOW CHRIST?

QUESTIONS FOR REFLECTION:

1. Do you think it is important to know Christ in the fellowship of His suffering? Why?

2. In what ways have, you suffered for Christ since becoming a Christ Follower. How does that compare to what Christ suffered for you?

3. What kinds of suffering in our world today do you think breaks the heart of God?

4. What can you do to make a difference in the lives of people who are suffering in our world today?

_____

_____

_____

_____

_____

_____

SECTION THREE:
THE POWER OF A SINGLE PRIORITY

Living In

THE POWER OF A SINGLE PRIORITY

The single priority for Living in the Power of One is *to love God with all of our heart and to love others as ourselves, and out of that love to touch the world with the love and message of Jesus Christ.*

When we love God with all of our heart, then we will be able to love other believers in spite of our differences. How the world is longing for the church to show love to one another and how the Savior wants us to quit warring among ourselves and to demonstrate a love that can only come from God for one another.

Living In

THE *Power* OF **ONE**

LOVING GOD AND LOVING OTHERS

Do You Love God With All of Your Heart and Others as Yourself?

The Gospel of Matthew records the conversation that took place between one of the religious leaders of the day and the Lord Jesus Himself. The spiritual leader asked Jesus what He thought was the most important commandment in the Law of Moses. Jesus replied with words that were clear, concise and compelling:

> *"You must love the Lord your God with all your heart, all your soul, and your entire mind. This is the first and greatest commandment. A second one is equally important: Love your neighbor as yourself. The entire law and all the demands of the prophets are based on these two commandments."*

> Matthew 22:34-40 NLT

Jesus declared that the world would know that we are His disciples, *by our love!*

Loving God With All Your Heart

When you love God with all of your heart, you realize that love is the key to a fulfilled and abundant life. God desires only one thing from us. He does not need our money, our talents, gifts, or our assistance, but He does desire our love!

To love God with all of your heart, we must understand:

- God is the *source* of all true love
- God *initiated* His love toward us
- God *demonstrated* His love for us
- God *pours* His love into our hearts through the Holy Spirit

The great natural wonder of Niagara Falls illustrates God's love. A massive amount of water rushes over the cliff and crashes onto the rocks below. As the water falls into the river below, a mist rises from the falls and ascends to the sky.

This is a beautiful picture of the love of God in our lives. We only can love God with all of our heart as *He pours out His mighty love into our heart.*

It is important to remember that:

	The more we	*know*	God
	The more we	*trust*	God
	The more we	*serve*	God
	The more we	*share*	God
	The more we	*love*	Jesus

Loving Others as Yourself

Jesus gave us the commandment to love others as ourselves, because we live in a world where people are starving for love, where self is king. People are interested only in themselves. This kind of lifestyle has created a love famine. Children, the elderly, teens, adults, the poor, and the rich are all starving for love.

Therefore, the Lord Jesus intends for His church and His followers to be a source of love to a world of hate, greed, and selfishness.

To love others, we need to remember, we love others because:

- God *first* loved us
- God *created us* to love
- Others *need* to be loved
- *God wants us to love*

If we are going to love others as ourselves, we must:

- *Start* with the **RIGHT ATTITUDE** which is **UNCONDITIONAL LOVE**

- *Build* on the **RIGHT FOUNDATION** which is **COMMITMENT**

- *Continue* with the **RIGHT APPROACH** which is **ACCEPTANCE**

Win Arn, the author of the book, *Ten Steps for Church Growth,*[11] gives us a definition of love that is very helpful and practical: *"Love is intentionally doing something caring or helpful for another person in Jesus' name, regardless of cost or consequence to one's self."*

Those who want to make an eternal difference make a priority of loving those whom God has put into their life:

- Family
- Friends
- Neighbors
- Colleagues
- Church Family
- The Needy Around Us
- Enemies

The Bible is very clear that loving others is more than just saying it.

---

[11] Ten Steps for Church Growth, Copyright 1997, Winfield C. Arn, and Donald A. McGavran, Harper Collins Publishers

We must demonstrate our love by actions. If you would like to demonstrate the love of Christ to others, I suggest some actions you may take:

- Make a love covenant with God
- Identify those in your life who need your love
- Do an act of kindness for those who need your love
- Communicate your love by saying it, writing it, showing it
- Actively look for love opportunities every day
- Give generously of yourself to those who are in need of love

THE BEAUTY OF GOD'S LOVE CAN FLOW THROUGH YOU TO A BROKEN WORLD.

QUESTIONS FOR REFLECTION:

1. How can you describe the love of God in your life? What things has He done to prove to you that He loves you?

_____

_____

_____

_____

_____

_____

2. How can a person learn to love God more? What steps do you need to take to love Him more?

_____

_____

_____

_____

_____

_____

3. How hard is it for you to love others? Which group is the most difficult for you to love?

_____

_____

_____

_____

_____

_____

4. Who are the people in your life that God would like for you to love? What will you do to begin the process of really loving them?

_____

_____

_____

_____

_____

_____

Living In

LOVING OTHERS

LOVING THOSE IN GOD'S FAMILY

An evidence that an individual has come to a personal knowledge of the Lord Jesus Christ is the fact that he/she sincerely loves others. This love is one of the great attractions to lost people when they see the love of God demonstrated in the lives of His people.

Jesus declared that the world would know that we are His disciples, not by our doctrine, not by our achievements, not by our titles, but instead by our love. *"Correct doctrine rarely attracts someone to a church. It is important to believe the right things, but the New Testament beautifully balances doctrine with teaching about how we should love one another and how we should behave toward each other."*[11]

Jesus gives us a *command* to love one another:

> *"I have loved you even as the Father has loved me. Remain in my love. When you obey my commandments, you remain in my love, just as I obey my Father's commandments and remain in his love.*

I have told you these things so that you will be filled with my joy. Yes, your joy will overflow! This is my commandment: Love each other in the same way I have loved you."

John 15:9-12 NLT

God desires that we, as His children, *demonstrate* His love to others.

John reminds us about Jesus' commandment to love one another:

"Dear friends, I am not writing a new commandment for you; rather it is an old one you have had from the very beginning. This old commandment—to love one another—is the same message you heard before. Yet it is also new. Jesus lived the truth of this commandment, and you also are living it."

I John 2:7-8 NLT

Then he challenges us to not to just talk about love but to reveal our love for others by our actions.

"Dear children, let's not merely say that we love each other; let us show the truth by our actions."

I John 3:18 NLT

Therefore, the question arises, how do we *show* love to our brothers and sisters in Christ?

The Scripture gives instruction on how we are to show our love to each other.

We are to:

- *Comfort* one another:
  "Therefore comfort one another with these words."
  I Thessalonians 4:18 NAS

- *Encourage* one another:
  "So encourage each other..."
  I Thessalonians 5:11 NLT

- *Build up* one another:
  "... build each other up, just as you are already doing."
  I Thessalonians 5:11 NLT

- *Seek what is good* for one another:
  "Show them great respect and wholehearted love because of their work..."
  I Thessalonians 5:13 NLT

- *Live in peace* with one another:
  "...And live peacefully with each other."
  I Thessalonians 5:13 NLT

- *Motivate* one another:
  "Let us think of ways to motivate one another to acts of love and good works."
  Hebrews 10:24 NLT

- *Confess* our sins to one another:
  "Confess your sins to each other and pray for each other so that you may be healed..."
  James 5:16 NLT

- *Pray* for one another:
  "...The earnest prayer of a righteous person has great power and produces wonderful results."
  James 5:16 NLT

- *Not to complain* against one another:
  "Don't grumble about each other, brothers and sisters, or you will be judged. For look— the Judge is standing at the door!"
  James 5:9 NLT

- *Not to judge* one another:
  "So let's stop condemning each other. Decide instead to live in such a way that you will not cause another believer to stumble and fall."
  Romans 14:13 NLT

- *Offer hospitality* to one another:
  "Cheerfully share your home with those who need a meal or a place to stay."
  I Peter 4:9 NLT

- *Prefer* one another:
  "Love each other with genuine affection and take delight in honoring each other."
  Romans 12:10 NLT

- *Edify* one another:
  "Let us therefore make every effort to do what leads to peace and to mutual edification."
  Romans 14:19 NIV

- *Accept* one another:
  "Therefore, accept each other just as Christ has accepted you so that God will be given glory."
  Romans 15:7 NIV

- *Help* one another:
  "We should help others do what is right and build them up in the Lord."
  Romans 15:2 NLT

- *Care* for one another:
  "This makes for harmony among the members so that all the members care for each other."
  I Corinthians 12:25 NLT

- *Greet* one another:
  "...Greet those who love us in the faith. Grace be with you all."
  Titus 3:15 NIV

- *Serve* one another:
  "For you have been called to live in freedom, my brothers and sisters. But don't use your freedom to satisfy your sinful nature. Instead, use your freedom to serve one another in love."
  Galatians 5:13 NLT

- *Submit* to one another:
  "And further, submit to one another out of reverence for Christ."
  Ephesians 5:21 NLT

LIVING IN THE POWER OF ONE CHALLENGES US TO MAKE A PRIORITY OF LOVING OTHERS.

QUESTIONS FOR REFLECTION:

1. How difficult is it for you to love other Christians
   in your life?

_____
_____
_____
_____
_____
_____

2. How difficult do you think it is for other Christians
   to love you? Why?

_____
_____
_____
_____
_____
_____

3. How can you make a conscious effort to live out "the love one
   another" passages in the Scripture?

_____
_____
_____
_____
_____
_____

4. Which ones are the easiest for you to do? Which ones are the hardest for you to do?

_____

_____

_____

_____

_____

_____

Living In

THE *Power* OF ONE

LOVING OTHERS WHO NEED CHRIST

How Can You Share the Love of Christ With Others?

Sometimes the church of the Lord Jesus Christ becomes so involved in secondary matters that it forgets its ultimate purpose is to share the love of Christ with others.

Jesus gave His disciples a great commission and a great commandment. What would happen if churches and ministries decided to become one in Christ with a single focus of fulfilling the Great Commission?

We could leverage our various gifts, talents, and resources to bring about a unified effort to reach multitudes of lost people for Christ.

The Lord Jesus Christ designed for the Church, to work together. **LIVING IN THE POWER OF ONE** challenge us to improve our connection to one another so that we can better reach the world.

One of the most critical dimensions of **Living In THE POWER OF ONE** is making an intentional decision for each of us to reach out to lost people. Our greatest privilege as a follower of Christ, is to reach another person who has never experienced the love of God in a personal way.

A survey was done several years ago among evangelical churches in America, and the results were staggering at that time and have only grown worse over the last few years:

- 85% of all churches in America are declining
- Only 1 church in 3 has any training ministry to help believers share their faith
- Only 2-3% of all Christians ever do anything about reaching a lost person
- Only 10% of those who are trained will ever do anything with it
- Most Christians do not have a lost friend

We often think of people who are sincere about reaching others for Christ as being just a little different from the rest of us. They can be obnoxious, offensive, or just plain strange. When we see those types of people, our immediate reaction is to say, "I do not want to be like that!"

While on the other hand, people who are great evangelists and reach many people for Christ are just a little different from us as well. They are saintly, holy, wise, gifted, fearless, and full of God. When we see people like that in our lives, our immediate reaction is to say, "I cannot be like that!"

The book, *Becoming a Contagious Christian*,[12] states *"that people who reach other people for Christ need not be weird nor must they be wonderful"*! They just have to love God and love others! How liberating that is for all the rest of us!

---

[12] Becoming A Contagious Christian, Copyright 1994 by Bill Hybels, Zondervan Publishing House, Grand Rapids, Michigan 49530

Living In

THE Power OF ONE

POWER OF ONE PROFILE

A Priority to Reach Out To Lost People

One of the most influential men in my life was my father-in-law, Dr. Robert Kline. When I accepted Christ as my Savior, he was my pastor, District Superintendent when I was a young pastor, and   General Superintendent. He was always a role model to me, and he was one of the wisest men I have ever known.

He taught me so much about the importance of family, church administration and leadership. However, his most significant impact on my life was his priority to reach out to lost people.

Sharing Christ with people was the joy of his life. Only eternity will reveal the people that came to Christ through his ministry.

While he was pastoring in Washington Court House, Ohio, he was instrumental in leading hundreds of people to Christ through a church bus ministry.

One Sunday morning as Dr. Kline was waiting in the church foyer for the morning worship service to begin, he noticed a little boy from one of the buses trying to open one of the doors into the church. The handle on the church door was just a little too high for him to reach. The little boy reached as high as he could. He stood on his tiptoes and reached as far as he could, but he could not reach the door handle.

Dr. Kline was moved with compassion, and went over to the door, opened it, and welcomed him into the church.

As the little boy entered the church, the boy flashed a big grin and said, "Gee, thanks Mister." Dr. Kline smiled back at him and told him that he was glad to do it.

At that moment, God spoke to Dr. Kline's heart. God whispered to him that many people would like to know Christ as their Savior, but the church world had put the handles of the doors too high.

He began to think about how the door handles are too high for average people to come to Christ. Some churches had dress codes that excluded people from coming, while others had traditions that unchurched people would never understand.

Other churches had developed sermons that the average person could not apply to their own life. Some churches did not take time to welcome new people to the church. Some of those people who came desperately needed an encounter with the living God.

As he made his way to the pulpit that morning to preach, God moved his heart to change his subject. He spoke that morning about the subject, "We Have Made the Handles Too High."

He preached with a broken heart. He wept as he talked to the church about making a new commitment to do whatever it took to bring the handles of the church down to where the average person could reach them. The church was challenged, and many came forward to pray with broken hearts about reaching out to people around them.

Because of his ministry and priority of his heart to reach out to lost people, the church grew from 400 to over 1,000 people. The church eventually bought 12 buses bringing in hundreds of children and adults. Finally, Dr. Stan Toler, who followed Dr. Kline as the Senior Pastor, constructed a new building to accommodate the number of people who came to the church.

The essence of **LIVING IN THE POWER OF ONE** *is* that every believer commits to reach one other person for the Lord Jesus Christ.

Do you realize what a difference we could make in our world if all of us decided we were going to reach one person for Christ in the next 12 months? We would see a spiritual revolution in our churches!

THE POWER OF ONE

THE POWER OF ONE IS a seminar, created by Dr. Stan Toler, focusing on how we can be effective witnesses for Christ. Stan taught what evangelism is and how you can become a bold witness for Christ. I have deeply appreciated his work on evangelism.

WHAT IS EVANGELISM?

Evangelism is a process of **COMMUNICATION**

Many people do not have a good understanding of who God is, what He is like, and how to have a relationship with Him. Evangelism is simply communicating these things to others in a way they can understand how much He loves them, how much He cares, and how much He desires to bring joy and meaning to their lives.

Evangelism produces **SPIRITUAL LIFE**

There are many service and social organizations in the world that bring physical help to suffering people. However, the Church has the privilege of sharing the gospel of the Lord Jesus Christ with people who are in despair. The gospel of Christ can not only help with physical needs but can bring spiritual life to an empty heart.

Evangelism meets **NEEDS**

As we look at our communities, we quickly realize that we live in a needy world. People have problems to face in their daily lives. Evangelism is finding a need and meeting it in Jesus' name.

*Evangelism **is SHARING THE GOOD NEWS***

Can you imagine someone finding the cure to cancer and then deciding to keep the news to himself or herself? It is unthinkable! Evangelism is sharing the best news that we have ever received! God loves us and sent His only son that we might have eternal life! Let us gladly share this good news with everyone we can.

*Evangelism brings joy when a **person ACCEPTS CHRIST AS SAVIOR***

Often, we think that evangelism is just living a good life or being a good person. Of course, that is part of our witness. However, evangelism brings great joy to the heart of God and to our own lives when we are able to lead another person into a saving relationship with Christ.

Stan also listed methods that he had used in building evangelism ministries in the churches he pastored. He suggested that some of these methods were:

- ***PRAYER: PRAYING FOR PEOPLE WHO ARE FAR FROM GOD.***

- ***NEEDS: DISCOVERING THE NEEDS OF PEOPLE AROUND US AND MEETING THEM.***

- ***RELATIONSHIP: BUILDING RELATIONSHIPS THAT ALLOW US TO SHARE CHRIST.***

- *EVENTS: PLANNING EVENTS THAT ATTRACT PEOPLE WHO NEED CHRIST.*

- *DEEDS: DOING GOOD DEEDS FOR OTHERS UNTIL THEY ASK WHY!*

- *MEDIA: USING MODERN TECHNOLOGY TO REACH OUT TO PEOPLE.*

- *WORSHIP: NOTHING IS MORE ATTRACTIVE TO OTHERS THAN AUTHENTIC WORSHIP.*

- *CHURCH PLANTING: NEW CHURCHES ARE OFTEN THE BEST WAY TO REACH NEW PEOPLE.*

Dr. Toler declared that evangelism must not be an optional plan of the local church. It must be an essential priority.

In order to share our faith with others who need to hear the good news of the gospel of Christ, let us determine to commit to the following action steps:

UNDERSTAND THAT SHARING YOUR FAITH WITH OTHERS IS BOTH A PRIVILEGE AND A RESPONSIBILITY OF EVERY CHRIST FOLLOWER.

CAREFULLY PUT TOGETHER YOUR TESTIMONY OF COMING TO CHRIST CONCISELY AND EFFECTIVELY.

You should be able to tell your story about what your life was like before you came to Christ.

You should also be able clearly tell how you came to Christ.

Finally, you should be able to share how much your life has changed since you must come to Christ

CAREFULLY IDENTIFY AND BUILD RELATION-SHIPS WITH THOSE WITH WHOM YOU WOULD LIKE TO SHARE YOUR FAITH.

Remember, in order to share your faith effectively with others you must *build a relationship with them first*! People must know that they can trust you before they will listen to you.

How can we find people who we can share our faith with and how can we build a relationship with them? Stan tells us to ask ourselves the following questions:

- Who are our neighbors?
- What is in their minds?
- Where can they be found?
- What are their interests?

BEGIN TO PRAY FOR THEM REGULARLY AND BECOME THEIR FRIEND.

- Pray for them daily
- Share four activities with them outside of the church next year
- Invite them to an event for the unchurched

DETERMINE TO SHARE THE LOVE AND MESSAGE OF JESUS CHRIST WITH THOSE GOD BRINGS INTO YOUR LIFE.

As you think of someone, you might be able to share the message of Jesus Christ with, remember Stan offers some very practical suggestions to help you to be effective. He explains that the process of coming to Christ is not complicated. He tells us that it is as easy as A.B.C.

A

Admit: *ALL OF US HAVE SINNED AND NEED GOD'S GRACE AND FORGIVENESS IN OUR LIVES.*

"For the wages of sin is death, but the free gift of God is eternal life through Christ Jesus our Lord."
Romans 6:23 NLT

B

Believe: *GOD REALLY DOES LOVE THEM. THEY CAN BECOME A CHILD OF GOD.*

"But to all who believed him and accepted him, he gave the right to become children of God."
John 1:12 NLT

C

Confess: *EACH ONE WHO COMES TO CHRIST MUST CONFESS HIM OPENLY WITH THEIR WORDS AND LIVES.*

> *"If you openly declare that Jesus is Lord and believe in your heart that God raised him from the dead, you will be saved. For it is by believing in your heart that you are made right with God, and it is by openly declaring your faith that you are saved."*
> Romans 10:9-10 NLT

COMMIT TO READ LIVING IN THE POWER OF ONE WITH THEM.

A person who makes a difference is a **STUDENT**

A person who makes a difference is a **STEWARD**

A person who makes a difference is a **SERVANT**

Living In

POWER OF ONE PROFILE

A Priority of Reaching Out to One Person

Many years ago, I heard a pastor tell an unforgettable story about the importance of reaching out to one person at a time with the love and message of Jesus Christ.

One Sunday morning at a church he pastored, a man who was slightly intoxicated heard the singing coming from a small church and it reminded him of his mother and his childhood many years ago. He stepped into the sanctuary and listened to the music, followed by a sermon. The pastor emphasized the importance of having a personal relationship with Jesus Christ and ended with a straightforward question, "If you died today, do you have the assurance of going to heaven?"

He stumbled forward to pray with the church counselors. During that time of prayer, he repented of his sins and asked the Lord Jesus Christ to come into his life.

He promised the Lord that morning that if God would forgive him of his sins, that he would devote the rest of his life doing something for God.

God, who is always faithful and true to honor His promises, did forgive him that morning and came into his heart. He was filled with a joy that he had never known before.

He gave thanks to God before the entire congregation. Then he remembered his promise to God: If God forgave him; he would devote the rest of his life in doing something for God. He then asked the pastor, "What can I do for God, now that He has forgiven me and has come into my life?" The pastor said that they would discuss it later. The old guy was still slightly under the influence of alcohol, so he refused to be silenced. He said, "No, I need to know right now something I can do for the Lord!"

He continued saying, "I remember when my mother was alive and how she always talked about giving a tithe to the Lord. What is a tithe?" Again, the pastor knew that it was not the time to discuss this in front of the entire congregation, so he replied, "It is a tenth." The man responded, "I do not know what that means, but I have two fifths in the car. Would that do?" Horrified the pastor said, "No, no that is not what I am talking about."

Finally realizing that the entire congregation was getting restless and wanted to leave, the pastor said to him, "Do you know anyone else just like you that needs to know the Lord?" The man said, "Oh yes, I know hundreds of them!" the pastor then said, "Go and find someone just like you and bring them to church with you next week."

Even though the man was under the influence of the alcohol, a light turned on in his mind. He said, "I can do that, and I will." Finally satisfied at what he could do for the Lord he allowed the pastor to dismiss the service.

When the next Sunday came around, the man returned and brought several of his old friends with him. They sat in the second pew so that they could hear every word.

When the pastor extended an invitation to receive Christ, the former drunk looked at one of his friends and said, "Come with me." He brought his friend to the pastor who stood at the altar in front of the church. He put his friend's hand into the hand of the pastor and said, "Here preacher, you save this one, and I will go and get another one."

That process continued until the entire row of former drunkards had come to a saving knowledge of Jesus Christ. The pastor and the whole congregation rejoiced at what had taken place, but they had no idea just how determined this new Christian was to keep his promise to the Lord.

The next Sunday, he brought one more person that he knew and again brought him to the pastor with the words, "Here preacher, you save this one, and I will go and get another one." For sixteen years until he died, every Sunday morning he brought at least one person to the pastor with the same words, "Here preacher, you save this one, and I will go get another one."

After I heard the pastor tell that story, I found a place to pray. I told God how sorry I was that with all my training, I had not been as committed as this dear man.

I asked God to forgive me for my complacency and to help me to realize the importance of reaching out to just one person.   It is my desire to do all I can to bring as many people as I can to the Lord during my life.

WHAT ABOUT YOU?

QUESTIONS FOR REFLECTION:

1. How difficult is it for you to share your faith with unchurched people?

2. What is more difficult for you, finding people to share your faith with or sharing your faith with others?

3. Who are the people in your life that God has given you a responsibility to share your faith?

4. Will you dare to commit to winning one person to the Lord Jesus Christ this year?

_____

_____

_____

_____

_____

_____

_____

SECTION FOUR:
THE POWER OF A SINGLE PURSUIT

Living In

THE POWER OF A SINGLE PURSUIT

The single pursuit for *Living In the Power of One* is *to pursue unity with other believers in the Body of Christ.*

Oh, what would happen in our community, our nation, and our world if the people of God would make it a pursuit to live together in perfect unity?

The Old Testament spoke about it. Jesus prayed about it. The early church experienced it. Paul taught about it. John witnessed it in the great city of God where people from every race, kindred, tribe and tongue will be gathered together for all eternity.

LIVING IN THE POWER OF ONE challenge Christians to make a sacrificial effort to live in unity with other believers.

If we are to live in biblical unity, we must make the following commitments.

Where there is	*vision...*	*declare it*
Where there is	*challenge...*	*accept it*
Where there are	*resources...*	*share them*
Where there are	*problems...*	*resolve them*
Where there are	*differences...*	*understand them*
Where there are	*hurts...*	*forgive them*
Where there are	*needs...*	*meet them*
Where there are	*people...*	*love them*

Unity does not just happen; we have to work at it. Often differences among people can lead to division, but this should not be true in the Church. Instead of concentrating on what divides us, we should remember what unites us. Building unity is the work of the Holy Spirit. He leads all of us to do our part to live in biblical unity.

Living In

THE *Power* OF ONE

BIBLICAL UNITY

Is It The Will of God For Churches to Work Together as One?

At first glance, this is a straightforward question with an easy answer. The obvious answer to the question is, "Of course it is!" However, from a real-life perspective, we know that this question poses a real issue for many churches.

The Word of God gives clear direction to those who wish to make an eternal difference in their life. In Hebrews 12:14 NLT we are told to *"Work at living in peace with everyone and work at living a holy life, for those who are not holy will not see the Lord."*

There are two significant challenges in this passage of Scripture:

The first is about living in peace with everyone.

It is my deep conviction that when the Church understands the importance of living in biblical partnership with other believers, we will be able to meet every need in our broken world.

You might say, do you think that the Church of Jesus Christ could meet *EVERY* demand in our society? My answer is a definite "YES"!

If the entire Body of Christ would merely link arms together to serve a broken world, I believe that there is enough workforce, money, assets, and compassion to meet every need.

The problem is that so many churches choose to live in isolation from the other parts of the Body. Many pastors and churches think that success is measured only by the size of the church or the ministries of one church. As a pastor for many years, I understand that kind of thinking. However, as I have matured and began to minister to the larger Body of Christ, I see how much good could come to our communities and our nation if we just merely linked arms together to serve our world.

John 17 is the great high priestly prayer of Jesus. In this prayer, offered just before His crucifixion, Jesus prayed for His disciples and for those of us who would follow in their footsteps. He prayed that His disciples would be protected, kept, and made holy. The very words that Jesus prayed in John 17:17-19 NLT were: *"Make them holy by your truth: teach them your word which is the truth. I gave myself as a holy sacrifice for them so that they can be made holy by your truth."*

It is clear that one of the distinguishing characteristics of a fully devoted follower of Christ is that he or she is to live a holy life.

No amount of work, zeal, or effort can take the place of holy living. We are called to be holy even as He is holy.

However, one of the aspects of a holy life is living in biblical unity with other believers. After Jesus prayed that His disciples would be holy, He then prayed that they might live in a sacred sense of unity one with another.

The prayer of Jesus was very intense and clear.

> *"I pray that they will all be one, just as you and I are one—as you are in me, Father, and I am in you. And may they be in us so that the world will believe you sent me. I have given them the glory you gave me, so they may be one as we are one. I am in them and you are in me. May they experience such perfect unity that the world will know that you sent me and that you love them as much as you love me." John 17:21-23 NLT*

LIVING IN THE POWER OF ONE is about what happens when fully devoted followers of Jesus Christ put aside their differences to minister to a broken world. The world is longing to see the Church come together as one to feed the hungry, heal the broken, reach out to the lost, bring good news to the hopeless, and demonstrate the love in a world filled with hatred and division.

What would happen in our communities if *The Church of Jesus Christ came together as one to serve the needs of our communities*? We would see an unprecedented number of people turning to Christ.

As important as THE POWER OF ONE is, we must realize that to make a real difference in our world, we *must link arms* with others in the body of Christ.

LIVING IN THE POWER OF ONE is not just about one individual effort, but about the difference we can make as Christians if we work together as one. The work of Christ multiplies when we *join hands* with others to accomplish our most important task.

One of us is never as good as all of us!

Those Who Make a Difference Realize the Importance of Working Together as One

The Bible tells us about the experience of the early Church in Acts Chapter 4. Peter and John witnessed a great miracle of a lame man made whole. The Jewish leaders interrogated them by what authority they had to perform such a mighty deed. Peter and John filled with the Holy Spirit and spoke these words boldly, *". . . by the name of Jesus Christ of Nazareth . . . this man stands before you healed."* Acts 4:10 NIV

The Jewish rulers then commanded Peter and John to never teach or preach in the name of Jesus again.

What would the early Church do in such a difficult circumstance? What would you or I do in the face of such threats? How do you think the modern Church would react?

The Bible tells us:

"As soon as they were freed, Peter and John returned to the other believers and told them what the leading priests and elders had said. When they heard the report, all the believers lifted their voices together in prayer to God..."

After this prayer, the meeting place shook, and they were all *filled with the Holy Spirit.* Then they preached the word of God with boldness. *All the believers were united in heart and mind.*

In addition, they felt that what they owned was not their own, *so they shared everything they had. The apostles testified powerfully to the resurrection of the Lord Jesus, and God's great blessing was upon them all.*"

Acts 4:23-24, 31-33 NLT

The early believers were living in such unity that they were *TOGETHER IN:*

- Prayer
- Possessions
- Heart
- Mind
- Blessing
- Grace

What was the result? The Bible says,

"There were no needy people among them. . ." Acts 4:34 NLT   Can you imagine it?

It is my sincere and passionate belief that when the Church of the Lord Jesus Christ works together as one, that we can see transformation of lives, communities, and even nations.

Oh, that we would learn the great truth of the importance of living in and working together in **THE POWER OF ONE** so that the world would know that Christ is the Savior of the world.

QUESTIONS FOR REFLECTION:

1. Do you believe that it is the will of God for all churches to work together in reaching out to touch the world with the love and message of Jesus Christ?

2. What do you think the Scripture means when it says that we are to *"work at living in peace with everyone"*? Hebrews 12:14 NLT

3. What do you think that Jesus meant when He prayed for His disciples to come to *"perfect unity"*? John 17:23 NLT Do you believe that the Body of Christ can experience this today? Why or why not?

4. Do you think that the early Church leaders thought the same about every issue even though they were together as one in Christ?

_____

_____

_____

_____

_____

_____

Living In THE Power OF ONE

POWER OF ONE PROFILE

Working Together To Meet Needs

In September of 1990, I accepted the call to serve as the Senior Pastor of the Brookside Church in Chillicothe, Ohio. It was my joy and honor to serve that great church for 25 years. One of the most amazing ministries of Brookside is the Food Pantry. Annually, they have served over 200,000 meals and are reaching out too many different communities with food assistance. Additionally, hundreds of people have come to Christ through sharing the love and message of Jesus Christ with those who come every week to receive food.

This ministry is truly making a great impact today, but it started with one person who felt that if we would work together as a church, we could do something significant for our community and for God.

Our first Christmas at Brookside, we gave out twelve baskets of food to needy families in our community. I was glad that we reached out to those twelve families.

I was giving my time and efforts in building the church; I did not evaluate what we did as opposed to what we could do.

A sincere and compassionate woman from our church called the church office and asked if she could set up an appointment. I agreed, and we established a time to meet.

When she came in, she seemed both happy and burdened at the same time. She stated that she knew, as a church, we had given out twelve baskets of food to needy families. I said that was correct and expected her to say how proud she was of us. However, the expression on her face changed to that of concern and she said, "I think we can do much better than that." I agreed but was not sure what she wanted us to do. I asked her, "What do you have in mind?" She said, "I think we need to start a Food Pantry."

A little shocked at her Food Pantry suggestion; I asked if she had ever started a Food Pantry. The answer was, "No." I asked if she wanted to begin a Food Pantry. Again, the answer was "No." She felt that certainly in a church our size, someone would want to do it. I said that there probably was someone, but we needed to pray about this together.

We agreed to pray about this potential ministry in the church. A few weeks later, I was talking with one of our older couples, Paul and Jean Dittman. I mentioned the conversation that had taken place between Kim and me. When Jean heard about this she immediately said, "Kim is right, and Paul and I are willing to begin and lead this ministry."

As it turned out, her uncle, Harry Bowers, from Grace Ministries Church, was leading a Food Pantry in South Columbus. Paul and Jean said that they would make an appointment with him and find out what we had to do to begin such a ministry. When they returned from that appointment several weeks later, they told me what we needed to do to start a Food Pantry and how to access government food from the Mid-Ohio Food Bank.

The Brookside Church Board gave their approval, and work began on this project. Paul and Jean turned a small room in our Fellowship Building into a food storage facility. They had help from a corporate sponsor who provided shelving. People in the church began to gather around the couple and said that they wanted to help with this new ministry.

Soon the day arrived for the Columbus Health Inspector to review our prospective Food Pantry to ensure that all governmental regulations were in place.

When he arrived, he said that our Food Pantry was one of the best facilities that he had seen in a while. He gladly gave his approval for us to begin. I then approached the subject that if we were going to use government food, "Would it be permissible to offer prayer, spiritual guidance, and material about the church during the hours of our operation?" He said that as long as we did not make it a requirement for the people to receive food, it was perfectly fine with him. That next Thursday, we began the Brookside Food Pantry Ministry. We did not advertise but just opened our doors. Remarkably, many families came to receive food assistance. It was both a heartwarming and heartbreaking experience all at the same time. Soon the word began to spread around the county that Brookside was operating a Food Pantry.

We were open one day per month, and the crowds began to overflow from our Fellowship Hall to our parking lot. People would come as early as 3:00 AM to park to get in line. We soon had to devise a traffic pattern that would allow them to wait in their cars for their place in line. Our Fellowship Hall could not hold them all.

It was during one of those mornings when the cars lined up entirely around the church that I was in my Office praying. I was praying that God would give us an opportunity to share the gospel with these dear people in a more effective manner than just giving them a gospel tract and information about the church.

It seemed that God stopped me from praying in this manner. He spoke to my heart and said, "I bring them to your parking lot, and they sit in their cars and wait for hours. What do you do?" Sheepishly I answered, "I go to my office." From that moment, I realized what a great opportunity this was for me. From that day on when the Food Pantry was open, I, along with many others, greeted the people in their cars. We offered to pray with them or share the love of Christ with them. It was a revolutionary ministry.

After Paul and Jean informed me that they were going to retire, a very talented and gifted (but timid woman) came to me and quietly said, "If no one else volunteers, I would be interested in leading the Food Pantry." I was a little shocked because I had never seen her as someone to take charge of this ministry. Something in my heart agreed with what she was saying.

Soon after that, Sandy Whited became the Food Pantry Director, and the results were incredible!

Our Pantry went from serving 90 families per month to over 200 families per week! After several years of serving, Sandy felt that it was time for her to retire from the Food Pantry. A man that I had known for over 40 years who had just recently recommitted his life to Christ, came to me and said that God had laid the Food Pantry Ministry on his heart. The Church Board gladly appointed Don Cozad and his wife, Linda, to the position.

Soon the ministry had expanded to serving the homeless and drug afflicted people who lived under a bridge as homeless people. After the Food Pantry would close each Thursday, leaders Don and Linda and several volunteers would take the Food Pantry truck and drive to a spot beneath the bridge.

People were a little skeptical at first, but after they learned they could trust them, people came from everywhere and of all ages—older people who could hardly walk, middle-aged people with children, and very young people who were battling with drugs, prostitution, and crime. We served every one of them with a smile and warm heart. I tried each time I was there to tell them how much they mattered to God and how much they mattered to me.

Soon our Food Pantry Team began to do more than serve food and meet people in their cars. Our Senior Adult Ministry led by Pastor Jack Norman opened their newly renovated Porter Senior Adult Center to those coming to receive food. Pastor Dan Bennett, who was on staff at Brookside, took the lead in ministering to this group of people spiritually.

He arranged to greet each person warmly, as well as offering a cup of coffee and some cookies.

He scheduled outreach days so that when the people came, they would see a Billy Graham film or other evangelistic events.

Pastor Dan Bennett trained Rev. Jessica Fout to stroll through the crowds, talking to those who came. She would often sit down beside someone in great need. She shared with them the beautiful love and message of Jesus Christ. Scores of people who came to receive food left with their sins forgiven and their lives transformed! Today, the Brookside Food Pantry still operates every Thursday, and they have now expanded to help other communities develop their Food Pantry Ministries.

It all started with one person who had enough courage to come to the new pastor in town and tell him that we could do better than twelve Christmas baskets of food.

WHAT IS GOD CALLING YOU TO DO? IT ALWAYS STARTS WITH JUST ONE!

Living In
THE *Power*
OF ONE

WHAT KEEPS CHURCHES
FROM WORKING TOGETHER AS ONE?

I believe, with all my heart, that if the Church today would learn to link arms together despite the things that separate us, God would once again fill us with His Holy Spirit, give power to our witness, and bestow great grace and blessing upon us.

Oh, that we would learn the great truth of the importance of living and working together again so that the world would know that Christ is, indeed, the Savior of the world.

If this is so, then why are churches not working together as one today?

As a pastor, I know the practical reality of why churches have a difficult time joining arms with one another.

There are genuine issues that must be acknowledged before churches can come together to serve a broken world.

A few of the differences that divide the churches are:

DOCTRINE

There are many in the Church that hold to different interpretations of Scripture. While the Bible serves as the only rule of faith and practice within the Body of Christ, many good and Godly people see the Scriptures from a differing point of view. These differing interpretations are not just opinions, but firm beliefs. The question then becomes, is it possible to work hand in hand with someone with whom we do not see eye to eye?

WORSHIP

There is nothing quite as divisive in the Church world than styles and preferences in worship. Some are very quiet and reflective while others are very exuberant. Some prefer old hymns while others prefer only the newest contemporary songs accompanied by a worship band. The list of worship differences between churches could be endless. I have concluded that the most challenging thing that the Church can do together is to worship together! The secret then for churches to come to a place of unity is to decide that it is not the gathering for worship that brings integration, but instead linking arms together to *SERVE THE COMMUNITY!* Serving others will bring us together in Christ.

TRADITION

Over the years, the various branches of the Church have developed traditions that are very sacred to the ones observing them but not observed by the entire Body. As a result, this can present some genuine tension within churches.

What happens when part of the Church feels very strongly about a tradition that they have observed or even heard preached from the pulpit while others completely disregard that tradition? This can cause division and separation within the churches. How can we overcome this problem and work together as one? Paul addresses this question in Romans 14.

Paul recognized that this possibility of differing traditions and opinions would surface in the Church. He knew that these things could either divide the Church or drive the Church to a deeper love relationship with God and each other. In this deeper love relationship, believers need to realize that all of us will stand before the judgment seat of Christ and give an answer for the things we have done.

Therefore, Paul admonishes us in Romans 14:12-13 NLT, *"Yes, each one of us will give a personal account to God. So, let us stop condemning each other. Decide to live in such a way that you will not cause another believer to stumble and fall."* What great advice! The question becomes, can I trust God to be the ultimate Judge of others while I continue to do what I understand to be right in my own heart and life?

COMPETITION

One of the realities within the Church, at least in the American Church, is that churches often feel a sense of competition. The lack of commitment by many church members give rise to fears that if various churches come together to serve the community, people will leave their present church to attend a new church. This concern is a genuine fear for many pastors and church leaders.

The only way to overcome this fear is to declare by faith that God is sovereign, and people belong to Him and not to pastors, churches or denominations. I know that this is something that is much easier to say than to do! Believe me, after pastoring for the last twenty-five years, I know that this fear is genuine. However, there are not very many good options available to address this issue.

One option is to try to keep a fence around our people and hope they do not get out or leave. I am not sure that attitude pleases the Father. While the other option is to step out in faith and believe that when we commit to serving to our community, God will bring to our fellowship the people we need and will subtract those who would be better somewhere else.

Positive Diversity

Considering all these issues, one would wonder if it is possible for the Church to work together at all! However, the truth is that God loves diversity! Instead of looking at differences between churches as a cause of division, what if we looked at them as different parts of the Body, bringing something unique to the table of grace. We can learn from each other and love each other in Christ.

Seeing churches serve together is a beautiful sight! It brings joy to the heart of the Father and serves as a reliable witness to the gospel of Christ to our communities.

Paul declared, *"Make every effort to keep yourselves united in the Spirit, binding yourselves together with peace."*

Ephesians 4:3 NLT

There are many good reasons for the Church to pursue biblical unity.

BIBLICAL UNITY IS EVIDENCE:

- Of the fact that we all serve the same God
- The same God lives in us all
- There is a purpose for spiritual gifts
- The Body of Christ is healthy
- We are living in the love of God

As followers of Christ, we should commit to pursuing unity with all our hearts in the following areas:

- Our Homes
- Our Church
- The Body of Christ in our Community
- Our Community
- Our Nation
- Our World

Building spiritual unity is one of the most critical roles of the Holy Spirit. He will help and guide us, but we must be willing to do our part of maintaining unity.

- We should live in a manner pleasing to God
- We should live with humility
- We should live in gentleness

- We should live by making allowances for others

- We should live doing our best to build unity:

Where there are differences, we must try to understand

Where there are hurts, it is essential to forgive

Where there are needs, let us attempt to meet them

Where there are people, let us love them

In our families, we pursue unity when we:

- Love Each Other

- Honor Each Other

- Respect Each Other

- Share With Each Other

- Work With Each Other

- Commit To Each Other

- Forgive Each Other

- Build Up Each Other

In our churches, we pursue unity when we:

- Focus on things that we have in common

- Be realistic in our expectations of each other

- Choose to encourage others rather than criticize

- Refuse to listen to gossip
- Support your pastor and leaders

In the Body of Christ, we pursue unity when we:
- Look for areas where we can work together
- Pray for a unified spirit
- Learn unity in prayer
- Commit to a unified purpose of bringing glory to God in all things

Often the reason churches cannot work together, and believers cannot live together in spiritual unity is because of conflict. I am convinced that one of the most significant issues in the church today is unresolved conflict(s) between one another. Therefore, if we are to work together as one, we must learn to resolve conflict with others in our lives. We will look at this subject in the next chapter.

THE BIBLE TEACHES ABOUT THE IMPORTANCE OF SPIRITUAL UNITY.

QUESTIONS FOR REFLECTION:

1. What do you feel are the most significant barriers for churches to work together in unity to serve a broken world?

2. Are you aware of any churches working together in unity that reach out to their communities? What are they doing together? How did they begin the process of working together?

3. In your opinion, how do churches overcome the differences mentioned in the study?

Doctrinal Differences?

_____

_____

_____

_____

_____

_____

Worship Differences?

_____

_____

_____

_____

_____

Traditional Differences?

_____

_____

_____

_____

_____

Competitive Differences?

_____

_____

_____

_____

_____

Living In

THE *Power* OF ONE

HOW CAN YOU RESOLVE CONFLICT WITH OTHER PEOPLE?

One of the things that continue to divide the Body of Christ is the presence of unresolved conflict and anger. The Church is so very human and sometimes can become a place of hurt rather than a place of healing.

The Word of God does not suggest that living together in unity will be an easy task!

Jesus never declared that we would not have problems or conflicts after we come to Him for salvation. The overwhelming evidence of the Word of God is that we all have different personalities, viewpoints, and opinions. So, how can we live in what Jesus declared as "perfect unity"?

It is important to remember that Jesus did not and does not call us all to be identical, but He does call us to live in unity.

One aspect of living in unity and avoiding unnecessary conflict is to develop some parameters for relationships *before conflict arises!*

While pastoring at Brookside Church, I developed a simple formula to help our church avoid unnecessary disputes. It was in working through conflicts that I began to develop this plan.

As I share this formula with others, there is almost a universal affirmation that could help avoid needless conflict. Out of my experiences of trying to resolve a dispute after it has developed, I share three simple concepts that can help avoid conflict.

Agreement:

Coming to complete agreement can be one of the most difficult and yet, one of the most important aspects of conflict avoidance. Agreement is the foundation of a working relationship. Agreement, at the beginning of a relationship or project provides a framework for discussion should misunderstanding or conflict occur later. An agreement is a difficult thing to achieve, but it is always more achievable on the front end than at a time when feelings are hurt, and misunderstandings have occurred.

Assumptions:

When people have done the hard work of developing an agreement, then the assumption automatically is that we will all live up to the things we agreed upon. However, when the work of agreement has not taken place, assumption becomes the framework of operation. One person *assumes* that things will be complete, or problems solved in the way that they think is best. The real question arises when good people have different assumptions about what actions will be taken.

In my experience, most conflict arises between good people when we live in the realm of assumptions rather than out of solid agreements.

Accountability:

Accountability is a popular word in the Church today. We love to speak about accountability, and we like to hold people accountable. However, where there is no agreement, there can be no accountability. Lack of accountability becomes a genuine source of conflict and, at times, can destroy a relationship or a project along with the people who are part of it.

The key to avoiding needless conflict is to make sure that you have come to *AGREEMENT* with those with whom you are working. Then, we can *ASSUME* that we will all live by the guidelines established in the agreement. Finally, when questions arise, or opinions differ, there is *ACCOUNTABILITY* to the covenant not to someone else's assumption.

It is my prayer that churches will understand the importance of the agreement, assumptions, and accountability.

The reality is that even when we have done all the work we can do at the outset of a relationship or the beginning of a project, conflict arises, and it ultimately must be resolved. We all have different personalities, preferences, opinions, and styles. It is inevitable that conflict will occur at the church as well as families, workplaces, and classrooms. The question then becomes how to resolve conflict when it arises in our lives?

The Lord Jesus taught us how to resolve conflict in Matthew 18:15-17 (NLT):

> *"If another believer sins against you, go privately and point out the offense. If the other person listens and confesses it, you have won that person back. But if you are unsuccessful, take one or two others with you and go back again, so that two or three witnesses may confirm everything you say. If the person still refuses to listen, take your case to the church. Then if he or she won't accept the church's decision, treat that person as a pagan or a corrupt tax collector."*

It is important to understand that the purpose of Matthew 18 is reconciliation! Broken relationships hinder the kingdom of God and the work of the Church in many ways.

RECONCILIATION:

The goal of meeting together with another believer is not to tell someone off, to vent about your feelings, or to bring their faults to light.

While these things may be a part of the process, we must remember that the end goal is to reconcile. We cannot stop just at venting our feelings without giving an opportunity for the other person to respond.

We cannot go into this process without acknowledging a problem has two sides and you may feel that the other person is entirely wrong, but you must agree to listen to discover what part you may have had in the conflict.

I once heard a Bible teacher suggest three questions that we must consider in reconciliation:

- What happened?
- How can we make sure that this does not happen again?
- Are we through with this?

When we have answers to these questions, reconciliation is possible.

The process described in Matthew 18:15-18 is:

- *GO PRIVATELY TO THE OFFENDER*

- *GO WITH SOMEONE ELSE TO THE OFFENDER*

- *GO TO THE CHURCH WITH THE OFFENDER*

- *FINALLY, TREAT THE OFFENDER AS A PAGAN*

The process that Jesus gives to us, as His people, is very clear:

The process must begin by going to another person privately. Most people will not take this step. We would rather go to others who feel sorry or be willing to fight for us. It makes us feel better when others tell how wrong the other person was.

Some people would rather withdraw from the person with whom they have the conflict and walk away. They never speak to that person again and never have any meaningful interaction with them. We write them off and decide to live life without them.

Ultimately, this becomes our only way to deal with a person that causes great pain in our life. However, this should not be the first response, but the last.

If we cannot make progress with a one on one meeting, then we are to take someone with us who could help mediate.

Someone to consider may be a mutual friend, a mutually respected leader, or even someone in an official position that could meditate.

If there is still no resolution, then we are to take the matter to the church, which most scholars believe is the Church Governing Board or Elders.

The Elders of the Church are the spiritual leaders of a church. One of their responsibilities is to listen carefully to both sides of a conflict and then give direction to both parties after prayer and discussion among themselves.

Once the Elders make a decision, then both parties need to submit to their wisdom whether they wholeheartedly agree or not.

Finally, if none of these actions brings reconciliation, then we are to treat them as a pagan, the one who has offended us.

Some might feel that this is a right to continue in a state of a broken relationship until that person makes things right with us.

However, consider how Jesus treated pagans. Jesus did not write them off or call fire from heaven down upon them. He prayed for them and even forgave them.

On the cross, the very first prayer of Jesus was, *"Father, forgive them for they know not what they do!"* Why would He pray that prayer? There was no evidence the people or the leaders had asked for forgiveness. There was no evidence that after Jesus prayed the people changed their behavior.

Then why did He pray, *"Father forgive them!"* It is my opinion that Jesus prayed to forgive them in order to keep His own heart from bitterness. The best way to protect our hearts from distress, pain, or resentment is to forgive those who have hurt us *EVEN IF THEY NEVER ASK!*

That sounds radical. It is! Nevertheless, Jesus came to give us a life of freedom and love. Forgiving those who have hurt us is one of the steps that brings freedom to our lives.

It is important to realize why this process is important in the life of the Church.

IT IS THE COMMAND OF CHRIST

We must remember as we read these verses that this is not some church policy statement, or the opinion of a preacher or leader, but the very command of the Lord Jesus Christ!

As our Lord and Savior, He commands us to live in unity with one another. He knows that it is impossible to live in this world without conflict and injured feelings.

Therefore, He commands us to follow through with this process. If the Church disciplined themselves to work through this, we would see a new sense of unity within the Body of Christ.

The Maxwell Leadership Bible details *A Case Study in Healthy Confrontation* in the Book of Philemon. This case study suggests several steps for us to take as we learn to confront conflict in a healthy manner:

- *PRAY* through your anger
- *INITIATE* the confrontation
- *BEGIN* with affirmation
- *ADMIT* you have a problem
- *EXPLAIN* that you do not understand what has happened
- *LET THE OTHER PERSON* respond
- *NARROW* the focus
- *FORGIVE AND REPENT* and do not stop until our hearts are transformed
- *COMPROMISE ON OPINIONS, NOT PRINCIPLES*
- *PRAY AND AFFIRM* as you leave

The theme of the Book of Ephesians is that believers are to *"lead a life worthy of your calling..."* Ephesians 4:1 NLT. Paul goes on to explain that one of the most critical aspects of leading a life worthy of our calling is to, *"Make every effort to keep yourselves united in the Spirit, binding yourselves together with peace. For there is one body and one Spirit, just as you have been called to one glorious hope for the future."*

Ephesians 4:3-4 NLT

Then, in one of the most powerful statements in the entire Bible about the importance of biblical unity, Paul says we must,

> *"...continue until we all come to such unity*
> *in our faith and the knowledge of God's Son*
> *That we will be mature in the Lord, measuring*
> *up to the full and complete standard of Christ.*
>
> *Then we will no longer be immature like*
> *children. We won't be tossed and blown about*
> *by every wind of new teaching. We will not*
> *be influenced when people try to trick us with*
> *lies so clever they sound like the truth.*
>
> *Instead, we will speak the truth in love, growing*
> *in every way more and more like Christ, who is*
> *the head of his body, the church.*
>
> *He makes the whole body fit together perfectly.*
> *As each part does its own special work, it helps*
> *the other parts grow, so that the whole body*
> *is healthy and growing and full of love."*

Ephesians 4:13-16 NLT

This passage of Scripture clearly defines what biblical unity is to look like. This is the picture of what Christ desires His bride, the Church, to look like.

Let us make every effort to see this come to reality in our churches and in the Church worldwide.

QUESTIONS FOR REFLECTION:

1. Why do you think living in unity with others is such a difficult task?

_____

_____

_____

_____

_____

2. What group do you have the most difficulty living in unity?

Family:

_____

_____

_____

_____

Church:

_____

_____

_____

_____

Body of Christ:

_____

_____

_____

_____

Community:

_____

_____

_____

_____

Nation:

_____

_____

_____

_____

World:

_____

_____

_____

_____

3. What steps could you take to pursue unity in each of the groups mentioned above?

_____

_____

_____

_____

4. Why do you think that unity is so important to God? To the Church?

_____

_____

_____

_____

Living In THE *Power* OF **ONE**

WHAT IS COMMUNITY TRANSFORMATION?

In 2014, I attended a Salt and Light Conference sponsored by EQUIP Ministries. The purpose of the Conference was to challenge us, as Associate Trainers who had trained over 6 million leaders in every nation on earth, to begin raising leaders for Community Transformation. This effort was to focus on the Body of Christ, serving as Salt & Light to communities all over the world. The Lord Jesus Himself introduced this concept when He told His followers in Matthew 5:13-14 NLT that they were to be *"The salt of the earth and the light of the world."*

It was at this Conference that I first heard the term, *Community Transformation.* I did not entirely understand what it meant, but it intrigued me. I thought it was a catchy phrase and something in which I could become involved. As I came to Ohio Christian University in the fall of 2015, I felt that God was laying a burden on my heart for this.

As I established The Toler Leadership Institute, I gathered a group of leaders around me. We began to discuss what Community Transformation might mean and how it might look. We considered three great questions:

1- What are the most significant needs in our community?

2- How could the Body of Christ truly be engaged to serve the community together?

3- How could the Body of Christ work with community leaders to address the needs?

The journey to understanding what Community Transformation is and how to move beyond discussion to action has been a most interesting one for me. It led our group to be honest and open with one another. It led me to face some tough but legitimate questions. It also led us to conclude we did not have all the answers, so we had to seek out others who had led Community Transformation in other locations.

The first person to help our group understand Community Transformation was Dr. John Maxwell. He provided the vision and dream of reaching out to the circles of influence in every community. He stated that if we were going to see a community truly transformed, we must engage the following influential groups in our communities:

The Church

The Family

The Educational Institutions

The Market Place

The Government

The Arts

The Medical Community

The Media

The second person that provided direction to our Community Transformation Team was Dr. Alan Platt. Dr. Platt has led Community Transformation movements all over the world. He began in South Africa with a deep burden to reach his city for Christ. He realized that he could not do it alone and one church could not do it by itself. This effort was going to require the whole Body of Christ within his city to come together to see the community transformed. He put together a Prayer Team and then followed God's direction. Churches came together, lives were changed, needs were met, and spiritual issues were confronted. He has written an excellent book, *City Changers: Being the Presence of Christ in Your Community,*[13] published by David C. Cook. This book has proven to be an enormous help to our team as we were trying to understand Community Transformation.

The third person that helped us understand the concept of Community Transformation was Dr. Terence Chatmon from EQUIP Ministries.

---

[13] Platt, Alan., City Changers, Published by David C. Cook, 4050 Lee Vance Drive, Colorado Springs, CO 80918, All rights reserved.

Dr. Chatmon had been part of a Community Transformation project in Chicago that produced remarkable results.

He said that as churches came together with business and community leaders, they were able to help begin new businesses, help people develop marketable skills, and build a sense of real community. This effort in community transformation saw the murder rate plunge 50% in an area of Chicago.

Based on what we have discovered, I now define Community Transformation.

The change that takes place in a community when faith-based leaders work together with community leaders to make a positive difference in their city.

Dr. Platt says that if we are going to get serious about this matter of Community Transformation, we must allow God to:

- *Change our mindset from concern to compassion*

- *Change our mindset from isolation to cooperation*

- *Change our mindset from activities to outcomes*

- *Change our mindset about being the presence of Christ in our community*

COMMUNICATE

COLLABORATE

CELEBRATE

- *Change our mindset from being withdrawn to engaging the community*

Dr. Platt also suggests a plan of action for church leaders to begin a Community Transformation initiative in their community:

A Process of Discovery

- *What are the needs?*

- *What is currently being done?*

- *Where is there a need for help?*

A Plan to Cover our Community in Prayer

- *Block by Block*

- *Hours of the Day*

- *Days of the Week*

If we are serious about the work of Community Transformation, then we must give ourselves to take intentional steps to bless our communities.

Try to discern what God is saying to your community

Make an effort to develop a team and a plan within your community

Do your best to engage the faith-based community

Commit to being Salt and Light to your community

QUESTIONS FOR REFLECTION:

1. What are the most significant needs in your community?

_____

_____

_____

_____

_____

2. How could the various churches in your community work together?

_____

_____

_____

_____

_____

3. How could the faith-based community work with civic leaders to bring positive change to your community?

_____

_____

_____

_____

_____

Living In **THE** Power **OF** ONE

MAKING A DIFFERENCE
WITH YOUR LIFE

How Can You Make A Difference
With Your Life?

This book is devoted to the premise that people who live with a single purpose, a single passion, a single priority, and a single pursuit can make a lasting difference in a broken world.

So the inevitable question is, *"How can I make a difference with my one and only life in this world?"* Unless you can answer the question with a sense of certainty, my suggestion would be to re-read the previous sections before moving forward.

Let's review the four main concepts of this study and make an action plan that will help you begin **Living In THE POWER OF ONE** on a daily basis to make an eternal difference.

LIVING WITH A SINGLE PURPOSE

Purposeful living is a commitment to do the will of God regardless of cost, consequence, or result. If you are going to make this purpose a practical and daily part of your life, I suggest that you commit, seek, love, and become a part of God's family.

COMMIT TO A SINGLE PURPOSE

COMMIT TO EXPERIENCE GOD'S AMAZING GRACE AND FORGIVENESS IN YOUR LIFE

We must understand to make a difference with our lives is *not attempting to earn God's grace and forgiveness. Rather, it is because of His forgiveness and grace!* This declaration should be relevant to all of us who want to do the will of God.

God is not against you. He is for you! He has done for you on the cross of Calvary what you could never do on your own. He paid the price for your sin and now accepts you as His Child. Let this assurance fill your life with joy and peace!

COMMIT TO GROW IN YOUR FAITH EACH DAY

Growth does not occur in a single day, but rather by the process of making it a priority to live it every day!

As we expand our thinking by reading, sharing, and learning each day, we begin to grow more and more into the person that God wants us to be. There is no substitute for this commitment of growth in your daily life.

COMMIT TO DISCOVER THE WILL OF GOD FOR YOUR LIFE

God desires for you to use your talents and spiritual gifts to make a difference in our world. Discover your spiritual S.H.A.P.E. and use the skills God has given you. Do not compare yourself with others or try to be someone that you are not! If your gift is serving others, then serve. If it is leading, then lead. If it is writing, then write. If it is encouraging others by a small deed of kindness, then help everyone you meet. The list goes on, and on...but the key is to discover how God has gifted you and *then use what He has given you to touch the lives of others.*

Do not worry if you feel your talent or gift is too small God couldn't possibly use you.

- Remember, the Bible has demonstrated over and over again that *God can use one person who is committed to making a difference.* Do not try to be something you are not. Be your best self and use whatever gift or talent that you have been given. God will use you to make a difference.

- Remember, we all have different and unique gifts and talents. If each one of us is using our spiritual gifts according to the will of God, together we will accomplish great things.

COMMIT TO A SINGLE PASSION

LIVING WITH A SINGLE PASSION

This passion is a passion for knowing Christ in the power of His resurrection and the fellowship of His suffering. To make this passion a part of your daily life, I recommend you:

SEEK TO KNOW CHRIST IN A PERSONAL WAY

One of the more revolutionary concepts of God is that He desires to be our *FRIEND*! He wants you to know how much you matter to Him each day. He wants to do life with you! He wants to be the One who encourages you, inspires you, understands you, and believes in you. You ultimately have no greater friend than the Lord Jesus Christ. Once you know this truth, your relationship with Him will never be the same.

SEEK TO BE FILLED WITH THE HOLY SPIRIT

Jesus said, *"But you will receive power when the Holy Spirit comes upon you."* Acts 1:8 NLT God has power for you to face whatever comes your way! He can cleanse your heart, give you courage, and overcome any obstacle that stands before you. Do not try to live your daily life without the power of the Holy Spirit at work in your heart.

SEEK TO UNDERSTAND THE DISAPPOINTMENT AND HEARTACHE OF LIFE IN THE LIGHT OF THE SUFFERING OF CHRIST

Disappointment and pain are a part of everyday life. These things do not come to destroy us, but rather to help us understand the heart of Christ more personally. We can learn to positively deal with disappointment. Jesus said, *"I have told you all this so that you may have peace in me. Here on earth you will have many trials and sorrows. But take heart, because I have overcome the world."* John 16:33 NLT

COMMIT TO A SINGLE PRIORITY

LIVING WITH A SINGLE PRIORITY

This priority is to love God and love others and with this love to touch the world.

LOVE GOD WITH ALL OF YOUR HEART

Remember, we can only love God with all of our heart if we allow Him to fill us with His overwhelming love. As He pours His love into our lives each day, then we are enabled to love Him in return.

LOVE OTHERS AS YOURSELF

What a challenge! Again, remember that we can only love others as God fills us with His love. We can love others who are different, who hurt us, offend us, and who challenge us. This is possible only through the supernatural power of God's love in our life.

SHARE THE LOVE AND MESSAGE OF CHRIST WITH PEOPLE WHO ARE FAR FROM GOD

Ask God to put someone in your daily path that needs to experience the love of God. Challenge yourself to express His love to people daily in some way—words, deeds, or prayers.

COMMIT TO A SINGLE PURSUIT

LIVING WITH A SINGLE PURSUIT

This pursuit is living in unity with others around us. It is such an essential piece of **Living In THE POWER OF ONE.**

We can make a difference with our one and only life, but we make the most significant difference when we link arms with others to serve a broken world. To make this pursuit part of your daily life, I urge you to:

BECOME A PERSON OF RECONCILIATION AND PEACE IN A TROUBLED WORLD

I first heard *The Reconciliation Song* at a Promise Keeper's Conference. It spoke to my heart about the need for biblical unity.[14]

The Reconciliation Song

> Oh let us be a generation of reconciliation
> and peace
> And let us be a holy nation
> Where pride and prejudice shall cease
> Let us speak the truth in love
> To the lost and least of these
> And let us serve the Lord in unity so others
> will believe.

---

[14] The Reconciliation Song| Writers: Morris Chapman, Clare Cloninger, Buddy Owen, Edward Owens,

BE A PART OF COMMUNITY TRANSFORMATION

The Church of Jesus Christ is called to be the salt and light in the world. *"Salt is good for seasoning. But if it loses its flavor, how do you make it salty again? You must have the qualities of salt among yourselves and live in peace with each other."* Mark 9:50 NLT

We must, as fully-devoted followers of Christ, be His presence in our neighborhoods, areas of influence, and communities. If churches are working together to influence community transformation, do your part. If there are no churches in your area working toward this priority, then be the one who introduces it. Remember transformation begins with one! Let that one person be YOU!

A new day is dawning for the church of the Lord Jesus Christ. It is a day when believers realize they can make a difference in the world by *Living In The Power of One.* We must recognize the strength that comes when we all work together for His Glory.

Let the Transformation begin!

Living In

THE Power OF ONE

The POWER OF ONE PROFILE

A Light in a Dark Place

She lives in one of the most broken neighborhoods in Columbus, Ohio. It is not far from the gleaming buildings in downtown Columbus and close to the new sports district, the Arena District. The wealthiest of the city drive by day after day but never seem to really see or understand. While I served as District Superintendent, The Churches of Christ in Christian Union purchased an old building in this area in 1985. The West Central District of the Churches of Christ in Christian Union renovated and used it for over 20 years as a transitional housing unit and an Inner-City Chapel that provided people with meals, blankets, and the gospel.

In 2009, Pastor Tim Tabor and his wife Beth, began a Sunday Evening Bible study for teens called, "The Home Church". Home Church was a safe place to have a meal, explore the possibility of faith in God, and learn to trust a Christian.

In 2011, Tim and Beth began taking people in their own home. These people were struggling with drug addiction.

In 2012, they opened their first Men's Ministry House. In February of 2013, they began a full-time recovery program, called C.O.M.O. (Compassion Outreach Ministries of Ohio) Recovery.

C.O.M.O. Recovery is a long-term, faith-based recovery program offering an 18-month program of healing and discipleship for people struggling with addiction and for those hopeless in spirit.

In March of 2013, with assistance from the Churches of Christ in Christian Union, they purchased the old Como United Methodist Church on Como Avenue in Columbus and began to restore it.

In 2015, they rented another house and opened a Women's Intermediate House. It was at that time that Tim and Beth invited their daughter and son-in-law, Taylor and Keith, to join the staff.

Taylor, a young woman, had graduated from Ohio Christian University with a degree in Disaster Management. Her dream was to be a missionary. She wanted to leave the United States and share Christ through holistic care around the world.

However, through her OCU experience, God pointed her in a different direction. God began calling Taylor to be a missionary in the United States. Her call is to serve in "the bottoms" of Columbus, Ohio, in that same building purchased by the denomination over 30 years ago. In addition to the Inner-City Mission, the Recovery Ministry purchased two additional houses adjacent to the old mission.

The Churches of Christ in Christian Union had long desired to develop a Safe House for young women who were caught in the horrible crime of sex trafficking. The property located in "the bottoms" provided a perfect space.

The ministry began to remodel the houses in order to serve both children and young women enslaved by traffickers. A local real estate company heard about this project and made it a focus of their community giving. Numbers of workers descended on the old houses to renovate, restore, paint, and repair them for ministry use. In October of 2018, The Respite House was ready to open its doors. There was no marketing campaign or grand promotion of this ministry. They simply held a Children's Fair and invited the neighbors to come. A large crowd came to enjoy the day, free from the horrors that was faced every day.

A week later, The Respite House opened for the first time. The purpose of The Respite House was to provide a safe place and shelter to young women who are victims of sex trafficking. My wife and I visited The Respite House in July of 2018. Tim and Taylor met us there and gave us a tour of the facility. The rooms were clean and there were comfortable couches for people to sit on. We noticed personal items that were given to any of the women who would stop by. We also noticed donated clothes and a changing room. The Respite House gave clean clothes, personal items, food to eat, and a place to rest to many young women. Connie and I both thought that this was so nice. Then we began to hear the real story.

Many of the women had been enslaved since they were small children. Many were abducted and given drugs by those who kidnapped them. The women become dependent upon their captors for food, shelter, and their daily fix for drugs. They had no hope and felt they could never escape. Many come with sores, cuts, bruises, and shattered hearts. The Respite House tries to help in a holistic way.

When I asked how many women come to The Respite House, Taylor responded, "About 40 per day". I was astounded! Their captors kept many of the women and even children in cages. In the middle of darkness as dark as I have ever seen, there is a light shining. The light is not The Respite House, but it shines out of it. The light is the light from the love of Jesus Christ shining through a small young woman by the name of Taylor and her staff.

She is at the house every day. She is there when the women come in. She is there to take their names and to tell them that they really do have value. She is there to bandage their wounds, help them with a shower, and provide them a few hours of dignity in an otherwise horror filled life. I asked Taylor how she maintained her own heart as she ministered to the suffering women. She said, "I know that God loves them and so do I". When I think of Taylor, I think of the old saying, *"When confronted by the darkness, some curse the darkness while others light a candle in the darkness."* Taylor and her family light a candle every day and the light shines in one of the darkest corners I have ever seen.

Very few have demonstrated *Living In The Power of One* more that Tim, Beth, Keith, and Taylor.

Living In

The POWER OF ONE PROFILE

The Power of One Person to Change a Community For Christ

In Mark Chapter 5, a fantastic story unfolds of how one man can influence an entire community for Christ. The story begins when Jesus had been teaching the people and the crowd became so large, that He had to enter a boat so that everyone could hear Him. It was a great scene as Jesus told simple stories that illustrated the good news of the Kingdom of God. *"As evening came, Jesus said to his disciples, 'Let's cross to the other side of the lake. "Mark* 4:35 NLT

The disciples may have been a little surprised because the people who lived on the other side of the Sea of Galilee were unclean. There were those who were not Jews and others who were engaged in filthy activities like keeping pigs! Most Jewish people avoided going to the other side of the Sea. The command of Jesus was clear, nevertheless, that He wanted to go to the other side. The disciples obeyed His command.

In the middle of their journey, a storm arose that threatened to sink their vessel. The disciples were terrified. They finally awakened Jesus with the cry, *". . . Teacher, don't you care that we're going to drown?"* Mark 4:38 NLT

Jesus then stepped forward and with a single word calmed the storm. The angry waves turned into glass. The disciples were amazed at the supernatural power of the Lord. When they arrived at the other side of the lake, a man by the name of Legion met them.

An evil spirit possessed Legion. He lived in the tombs and could not be restrained, even with chains. The Bible says,

> *"Whenever he was put into chains and shackles—as he often was—he snapped the chains from his wrists and smashed the shackles. No one was strong enough to subdue him. Day and night, he wandered among the burial caves and in the hills, howling and cutting himself with sharp stones."* Mark 5:4-5 NLT

When Jesus met Legion, the evil spirits that possessed him, asked the Lord not to destroy them but to allow them to enter a herd of swine feeding nearby.

The Bible then records,

" So, Jesus gave them permission. The evil spirits came out of the man and entered the pigs, and the entire herd of about 2,000 pigs plunged down the

steep hillside into the lake and drowned in the water." Mark 5:13 NLT

The herdsmen ran to the nearby town telling of the miracle they had seen. To their utter amazement, they found him, *"A crowd soon gathered around Jesus, and they saw the man who had been possessed by the legion of demons. He was sitting there fully clothed and perfectly sane, and they were all afraid."* Mark 5:15 NLT

Upon seeing this strange, yet wonderful sight, the townspeople began to plead with Jesus to go away and leave them alone. As Jesus was getting into the boat to leave the area, Legion came to Him and begged to go with Jesus. Jesus responded saying, *". . . No, go home to your family, and tell them everything the Lord has done for you and how merciful he has been."* Mark 5:19 NLT

In obedience to the command of Christ, Legion began to travel everywhere in the region gladly proclaiming what the Lord had done for him. The Bible says that everyone was amazed at what he said. What a beautiful story, but that is not the end!

After the death of John the Baptist, Jesus wanted to cross over again to the other side of the Sea of Galilee. He sent His disciples ahead of him in the boat while He stayed to pray on the mountainside. Late that evening another storm arose.

Jesus could see from the mountain that His disciples were in serious trouble. They were rowing hard and struggled against the wind and waves.

About three o'clock in the morning Jesus came to them walking on water.

"But Jesus spoke to them at once. 'Don't be afraid,' he said. 'Take courage! I am here!' "Mark 6:50 NLT. When Jesus boarded the vessel, they found themselves safe on the other side of the Sea in the same area where they had met Legion sometime before. However, this time the greeting was completely different. This time, "*...the people recognized Jesus at once, and they ran throughout the whole area, carrying sick people on mats to wherever they heard He was. Wherever he went—in villages, cities, or the countryside—they brought the sick out to the marketplaces. They begged him to let the sick touch at least the fringe of his robe, and all who touched him were healed.*" Mark 6:54-56 *NLT*

What made the difference in an entire region that had been hostile to Christ? The answer is to be found in the life of one man, Legion. Jesus had delivered him from the evil spirits. This one man then began to tell his story everywhere he went. As the people listened, fear was forgotten and replaced with hope. Perhaps, Jesus would one-day return to their region. If He ever returned, people believed that if He could heal Legion, He could heal them!

What a sight it must have been that day as many people brought their friends and loved ones just to touch the hem of the Master's garment to be healed. All of the praise of heaven echoes through in words, *"AND ALL WHO TOUCHED HIM WERE HEALED."* Mark 6:56 NLT

WHEN ONE PERSON LIVES IN THE POWER OF ONE AN ENTIRE COMMUNITY CAN BE CHANGED.

QUESTIONS FOR REFLECTION:

1. Most concisely and straightforwardly as you can, describe what **Living In THE POWER OF ONE** is about and how it can make a difference in your life?

   _____

   _____

   _____

   _____

2. As you reflect on the power of a single purpose, what seemed to stand out to you?

   _____

   _____

   _____

   _____

1	2	3	4	5
Not at all	Very Little	Neutral	Somewhat	Mostly

3. Using the scale above, where you would rate yourself about living with a single purpose of doing the will of God regardless of cost, consequence or result?   Why?

   Rating Number_____

   _____

   _____

   _____

   _____

4. As you reflect on the power of a single passion, what seemed to stand out to you?

_____

_____

_____

_____

_____

1	2	3	4	5
Not at all	Very Little	Neutral	Somewhat	Mostly

5. Using the scale above, where would you rate yourself on how well you know Christ and experience His power and suffering? Why?   Rating number: _____

_____

_____

_____

_____

6. As you reflect on the power of a single priority, what seemed to stand out to you?

_____

_____

_____

_____

7. On the following scale below of 1-5, where would you rate yourself on:

1	2	3	4	5
Not at all	Very Little	Neutral	Somewhat	Mostly

Loving God, and why?   Rating number: _____

_____
_____
_____
_____

Loving Others, and why?   Rating number: _____

_____
_____
_____
_____

Loving Lost People, and why?   Rating number: _____

_____
_____
_____
_____

8. As you reflect on the power of a single pursuit, what seemed to stand out to you?

_____
_____
_____
_____
_____

9. On the following scale of 1-5, where would you rate yourself on your commitment to:

1	2	3	4	5
Not at all	Very Little	Neutral	Somewhat	Mostly

Pursuing a single pursuit, and why? Rating number: _____

_____

_____

_____

_____

_____

Pursuing a holy life, and why?   Rating number: _____

_____

_____

_____

_____

Pursuing living in Biblical unity with others, and why?
Rating number: _____

_____

_____

_____

_____

_____

_____

_____

Living In

JESUS: THE POWER OF <u>THE</u> ONE

Never in human history has there been another like Jesus of Nazareth. He stands unique among all who ever have lived or ever will live. He towers above every king, ruler, philosopher, or leader. There is no one like Jesus.

He proved that He is <u>The</u> One by His:

- Virgin Birth
- Virtuous Life
- Vicarious Death
- Victorious Resurrection
- Promised Visible Return

Oh, my friend, Jesus is The Power of <u>THE</u> One. If any of us can accomplish any good in our lives, it is because we reflect His Grace and Mercy in a fallen world. He is the One who has made the ultimate difference in history. He is the One who can transform our lives. He is the only One who transforms churches, and He is the only One who can bring about cultural transformation.

HE IS...

- Only begotten of the Father full of Grace and Truth

- The Way, the Truth, and the Life and no one comes to the Father but by Him

- The Eternal and Everlasting Word of the Father

- The King of glory and bears a name, which is above all names

- The Bread of Life

- The Good Shepherd

- The Door to Eternal life

- The Resurrection and the Life

- The Alpha and Omega, the Beginning and End

- The Stone that the builders rejected, but the Cornerstone for all who believe

- The Almighty God, the Wonderful Counselor, and the Prince of Peace

- The Rock of all ages

- The Savior of the world especially to those who believe

- The Light of the world

- The Spotless Lamb of God who takes away the sin of the world

- The Redeemer

- The Coming King

- The Author and Finisher of Our Faith

As we conclude this study, let us bow before Him and seek His presence and power in our lives. The highest honor to any human on earth is to reflect the strength of THE One to those who are in desperate need.

The good news is that He loves us and is willing to transform our lives and to help bring transformation to others. If you desire to **Live In THE POWER OF ONE,** you must come to know, in a personal way, THE One who can do more than we could ever ask or imagine.

To Him be all Glory in the Church and the world forever. Amen.

TODAY I COMMIT TO...

A SINGLE PURPOSE: To do the will of God regardless of cost, consequence or result

A SINGLE PASSION: To know Christ better

A SINGLE PRIORITY: To love God and love others

A SINGLE PURSUIT: To build unity in the Body of Christ

Signed: _____

Date: _____

THE STAN TOLER LEADERSHIP WORKSHOPS

The Vibrant Church

The Exceptional Leader

The Five Star Church

Outstanding Leadership

The Power of One

Total Stewardship

Teaching to Influence Lives

The Relational Leader

Total Quality Life

Give to Live

The Power of Your Attitude

Terrific Customer Service

Holiness: Reflecting the Heart of God

ABOUT THE AUTHORS

 Rev. David Dean currently serves as the Director of Evangelism for the Churches of Christ in Christian Union. He has been an influential leader for the cause of Christ for many years. As a life-long friend to Dr. John C. Maxwell and Dr. Stan Toler, he has learned about effective church leadership from some of the most acclaimed leaders in the church world today.

He served the Brookside Church in Chillicothe, Ohio for 25 years as the Senior Pastor. He pastored three other churches in Tucson, Arizona; Alma, Georgia; and Urbana, Ohio. He has also served as a District Superintendent, University Church Relations Director, Executive Director for the Toler Leadership Institutes at Ohio Christian University and EQUIP Associate Trainer.

His ministry has taken him across the United States and into 26 foreign countries preaching and teaching the gospel of Christ.

His passion is to see the Church of the Lord Jesus Christ be strengthened and to reach out to lost people around the world.

Stan Toler was a dynamic international speaker, having spoken in over 90 countries of the world. He has written more than 100 books, selling more than 3 million copies worldwide, including his best-sellers, The Secret Blend, The Relational Leader, The Exceptional Leader, ReThink Your Life, his popular Minute Motivator series, Total Quality Life and TERRIFIC! Five Star Customer Service.

For many years, Toler served as Vice-President and taught seminars for John C. Maxwell's INJOY Leadership Institute, training church and corporate leaders to make a difference in the world.

Called into ministry at a young age, Dr. Toler preached approximately 15,000 sermons to over 200 denominations in all 50 states and 80 different countries. In his more recent years, Dr. Toler pursued his passion for non-profit ministry through his foundation, Toler Leadership International, attempting to train the next generation of young, Christian leaders.

Serving as a pastor and General Superintendent in the Church of The Nazarene, he is most widely known for his career as an author, merging his life of faith with his knowledge of leadership by publishing throughout his career.

He not only influenced other's lives through his words, he influenced others through his posture of faithfulness and devotion.

Made in the USA
Columbia, SC
21 February 2020

Rev. David Dean currently serves as the Director of Evangelism for the Churches of Christ in Christian Union. He has been an influential leader for the cause of Christ for many years. As a life-long friend to Dr. John C. Maxwell and Dr. Stan Toler, he has learned about effective church leadership from some of the most acclaimed leaders in the church world today.

David serves as a Director for Toler Leadership International. This organization is committed to raising up effective, Godly leaders around the world.

LIVING IN THE POWER OF ONE IS DESIGNED TO ENABLE YOU TO MAKE A DIFFERENCE IN A BROKEN WORLD WITH YOUR ONE AND ONLY LIFE!

Dr. Louie Bustle first introduced this concept while serving as a Field Director for the Church of the Nazarene in South America. It brought much enthusiasm and growth to churches in South America.

Dr. Stan Toler then developed this concept in a seminar entitled, The Power of One. This seminar focused on the importance on the work of evangelism. It brought a renewed passion for reaching out to lost people to the church he pastored in Oklahoma City, as well as to churches around the world.

Dr. Stan Toler personally asked Rev. David Dean to write a companion book to The Power of One, which would focus on evangelism and discipleship. Living In The Power of One is that book.

LIVNG IN THE POWER OF ONE CHALLENGES YOU TO MAKE AN ETERNAL DIFFERENCE IN OUR WORLD.
ARE YOU READY FOR THE CHALLENGE?

ISBN 9781089547815

90000

9 781089 547815